Memories

LAUGHTER

&GARLIC

Jewish Wit, Wisdom, and Humor
to Warm Your Heart

Including A Glossary for the "Yiddishly Challenged"

LEO LIEBERMAN

COMTEQ
PUBLISHING
MARGATE, NEW JERSEY

Published by:
ComteQ Publishing
P.O. Box 3046
Margate, New Jersey 08402

Library of Congress Catalog Card Number: 99-65809
Lieberman, Leo
Memories of Laughter & Garlic – Jewish Wit, Wisdom, and Humor To Warm Your Heart
Including a Glossary of Conversational Yiddish
240 p. cm
ISBN 0-9674074-0-0
1. Self Help
2. Inspiration

Graphic design and layout: Rob Huberman
Cover art: Scott Petinga

Printed in the United States of America
10 9 8 7 6 5 4 3 2 1

These memories are for all the children who did not experience "the olden days" first-hand. So, in the hope that those days will not fall into a cave where no one enters, I dedicate this book to them.

To all the Rachels and Marks

To all the Micahs, Laurels, Aris, and Tamars

To the Jasons and Joshuas

To the Vanessas and Maxies

And to those whose presence permeates these pages and who have been a source of inspiration.

And to all our children and grandchildren.

And especially to all the Tanta Peshas of this world.

And to all of you, the readers...this book is lovingly dedicated.

Acknowledgements

To a very good part, this book has resulted from the support and encouragement of the staff at the *Jewish Times of South Jersey*, where my newspaper feature column "Chalk Dust" has been running weekly since 1997.

A special thanks to *Jewish Times* publisher Shy Kramer for his support and encouragement and who lent me his sage advice and the much needed pat on the back. He was one of the first people who recognized the need for preserving the past as connection to our heritage and I am most indebted to him.

To Rob Huberman, *Jewish Times* Managing Editor, who provided not only his friendship, but who also worked relentlessly to edit my essays, improve the format of my columns and turn them into a book, and who helped me along every step of the way, I can never adequately express my appreciation to him, except to say that he knows how much his help has meant to me.

To the ladies, Ann, and Janet and Laura…all three 'Women of Valor,' reminiscent of the Book of Proverbs. Their love led the way as did their suggestions and comments.

To Sharon Linker, for taking time on weekends to help with the manuscript and for helping those of us who are 'computerly challenged' with those aspects that are so sorely needed.

To my readers, supporters, and friends who told me how much *Chalk Dust* has become part of your lives, I gratefully salute you.

And to YOU who will read this book and pass along a copy to a friend, a relative, a child or a grandchild, I acknowledge you and give you my appreciation and affection.

CONTENTS

1. Life's Little Lessons

2. All in the Family

3. Growing Up Jewish

4. Old Times in the Old Jewish Neighborhood

5. Celebrating Jewish Style

6. School – More Than an Education

7. Nu? So, What Else Is New?

8. Glossary of Conversational Yiddish

Preface

Simply put, reading Leo Liebermen is like going back home to Bubbe – revisiting a world of long-lost *Yiddishkeit* when all was warm and cozy and the shtetle still alive even here in America.

But you don't necessarily have to be Jewish to love "Memories of Laughter and Garlic." If you appreciate good writing, wit and wisdom – sprinkled with Yiddishisms reminiscent of Sholom Aleichem – this book is for you.

Lieberman consistently manages to keep things fresh – indeed, as if he'd gone back to Bubbe for more material.

But of course, it's Lieberman's world, a world some of us still remember with great fondness – and in case we forget – that's where Lieberman comes in, to bring it all back. If not for our Leo Liebermans, a significant portion of our cherished past would no longer even be a memory. For that reason, all humor aside, this collection is essential.

Lieberman's style is so deceptively simple that many readers probably don't know that this man is a professor – an intellectual, *noch!*

That, of course, is precisely Lieberman's gift – away with pretense and ostentation! If you think you're a *macher*, Lieberman's Tante Pesha will swiftly cut you down to size.

Some say that Yiddish, as a language, is dying out. Maybe yes, maybe no. But without question Yiddish inflections have enriched the English language. Take, for example, the commonly used phrase, "Enough already," which comes from *genuge shoyn*. So if you need a translation of any Yiddish expression in this book, just flip to the back and check out Lieberman's "Glossary for the Yiddishly Challenged."

Anyway, the phrasing that charmingly turns English into Yiddish (or is it Yiddish into English?) comes up frequently in this work, as Lieberman has Mama say: "If your Papa had to chose between me and his checkers – better not ask!"

If forced to use one word to define this entire work, I'd go with "charm." I would not dare say that Lieberman's essays are vital in preserving Jewish heritage – are you kidding?

Tante Pesha would only laugh and say, "Such a big deal from my Leo? *Ay yi yi!*"

Jack Engelhard, Author
"Indecent Proposal"
"Deadly Deception"
"The Days of the Bitter End"

Introduction

There is a saying that, as a people, we are held together with a sense of memory. So it is, that the most solemn day of the year is sometimes called Yom Ha-Zicaron – the Day of Remembrance.

Now don't get worried – you won't need a dictionary or a knowledge of Hebrew or Yiddish (still...) to enjoy this book. (You might need a sense of humor, though. But not to worry – if you don't have that, you will most likely develop one before you get half-way through!)

But back to our topic. I once attended a rally in Manhattan (that's in New York – and some say _that is_ New York!) and there were hundreds, maybe thousands of people all wearing buttons and carrying signs with the one word: "REMEMBER." We were being told not to forget the millions of people – men, women, and children...Jews, Righteous Gentiles, Gypsies, handicapped – who were slaughtered by the Nazis.

We are reminded in the Good Book to remember Amalek and what he did; how he used treachery against the Israelites. Well, this book, too, is remembrance, a sense of memory.

But must all memory be mournful? Must remembering always have such sad or doleful undertones, a music written in a minor key and etched into our psyche? I think not.

Memory contains a leavening of humor, of smiles, and even giggles. Admittedly, it is sometimes laughter through tears, but there is always the laughter – and the need not to take ourselves too seriously on every issue.

Remember the kid who came running home to announce to his grandfather, "Grandpa – *Zaydie* – did you hear? Did you hear the news?" And Grandpa looked up, confused, and the little boy continued, "The Dodgers just won the pennant! What do you think?!"

And the elderly *Zaydie*, looked up from his newspaper and asked, "So what does it mean for the Jews?"

And once, when Mama was past ninety and she was asked if she had any advice for those who wanted to live to a "ripe old age," she offered the following suggestion: "Every day you must eat a clove of raw garlic and also have one good laugh!"

Now I must admit that once in a while I forget the garlic clove. But the laugh...never!

So don't take yourself too seriously. Just keep turning these pages and keep remembering – the happy as well as the serious. Both are important.

And be prepared to meet some very special people. Of course there will be Mama, and Uncle Maxie, and Lilly With The Nails, and Abie From The *Shul*. And there's Fat Rosie From Apartment 3-C, and the rabbis and teachers, the Principal, and the Professor (after all, I've been a teacher for well over...never mind. Age is only a number. And who needs to count?) And especially there will be the one and only Tanta Pesha!

And in case you're wondering if you have to be Jewish to enjoy this set of memories – of course not, although it wouldn't hurt, either.

But enough already with this philosophy and this introduction. The proof of the noodle pudding is in the eating. So turn the pages and read. And, above all, enjoy!

1. Life's Little Lessons

Ari — A 7-year-old Grapples With the Holocaust.

"Why didn't someone stop them?"

He's only a little guy with a mop of red-blond hair sitting on top of a pixie-ish face that contains a smile (devoid of a few front teeth) that calls for a hug. He's seven years old and like all seven-year-old boys, he's a perpetual motion machine, always moving, running, jumping, making catches with imaginary balls, and always succeeding in tossing the nonexistent ball into that nonexistent hoop and then jumping up as his ears catch the roar of the crowd.

His name is Ari, and in case I forgot to mention it, he also happens to be my grandson—one of four grandsons and flanked by four granddaughters. So of course, he's very special.

And so one day when the phone rang and I picked it up on the second ring, I was delighted to hear the little voice at the other end of the line telling me that it was Ari. (Although I certainly had already guessed when he greeted me with the usual "Hello Grandpa" voice.)

And today there was a special request. "Grandpa, could you do me a favor?" I didn't wait for a heartbeat to elapse before I informed him that whatever he wanted was his, even if it were for half my kingdom. (And this wasn't even Purim!)

It wasn't half my kingdom that he desired. All he wanted was to have me come over and be with him. Could I refuse? Down went the books. Off went the computer. On went the sweat shirt with the hood. And I arrived like the morning milk at his doorstep.

And so we decided—just we two guys, (sometimes it's good to get away from three siblings and a mother and father)— to go on a treasure hunt. And what better place than the beach!

We were both in agreement, and after announcing our plans, we headed down to the beach. Here we discovered a wealth of treasures. Sometimes it is I who makes the discovery of a piece of driftwood that looks just like a bird; and sometimes it's Ari who spots a conch half concealed under a mound of sand. And as we run (he runs, I walk) there's an occasional wave that threatens us if we get too close to the water's edge.

But so what? What are wet socks when the sun is shining and the sky is blue and the sand tickles your feet if you dare (double-dare with a "d") to remove your shoes?

And I must admit that I am taken by surprise when this seven-year-old looks at me and asks, "Grandpa, why did they kill so many people?"

I take a deep breath while he continues, "Why, Grandpa? They weren't hurting anyone. Just because they were Jewish. Why should they be killed? Even little children. Why didn't someone stop them?"

I try to think of a suitable answer, but none comes to my lips. What can I answer? Shall I tell him to ask his father? His mother? The Rabbi? All I can say is, "I don't know either."

But Ari isn't satisfied with this admission of ignorance and he keeps on. "Grandpa, you know everything. You're a teacher. At college. You teach people all about what happened."

A pause from both of us and then from him, "So why?"

I can't answer and I won't give him a stock reply of "some Divine Plan" or some response that I don't believe. So all I can do is scoop him up in my arms, treasures and all, and hug him.

We continue our walk, holding each other's hand. The treasures are saved in a plastic bag and the sky is still blue and there are small birds on the beach. And it is such a day like this that caused the poet to exclaim, "God's in His heaven; all's right with the world."

But I squeeze the seven-year-old hand even tighter and he looks at me and says, "Don't be sad, Grandpa. We won't let it happen again when I grow up, will we?"

I suddenly become aware of my own mortality, my own shortcomings, and all I can answer is, "I certainly hope you're right."

And I dab a tear from my eyes, telling Ari that some sand must have gotten into them.

Defending Against Those Jewish Calories — Mama's 5 Tips

"Eat only when standing up."

I remember – oh how I remember – growing up with the belief that if I didn't finish every morsel on my plate, there would be some cute little baby somewhere in China (or was it India? No, I'm sure it was China.) who would suddenly and mysteriously die of starvation.

I didn't question this belief. I accepted it knowing that Mama would never misrepresent (that's a nicer word than "lie"). And so I forced down all the carrots and all the spinach (the latter would give me muscles in addition to saving that Chinese tyke) and I drank all my milk (good for the bones and teeth).

And then one day I grew up and looked in the mirror and stepped on the scale. Could the scale be correct? I pulled in my belly and took a deep breath. The little hand on the scale did not budge. (No, I shall not reveal the numbers.)

And I also learned that I was not alone with this problem. Inside of every fat fellow there's a skinny guy yearning to emerge. Or is it the other way around? Whatever. But today as I read all those articles written by the Cherubic Chef, the Galloping Gourmet, and the Bucolic Baker, I feel certain that the internal skinnies haven't a chance. The world is filled with delicious chocolate fondues, scrumptious cream sauces, and lots of cafe *mit schlag – mit* lots of *schlag.*

So here comes the problem – how can we defend ourselves against the horde of invading calories tempting us like the centerfold of that magazine, seducing us with honeyed *(oy,* more calories) words like, "Only a little – no one will know."

But all too soon we complain that the new shirt is cut too small and the dungarees that used to be so comfortable were probably not sanforized and so shrank in the washing machine. And, *oy vay,* what happened to my knees? They were here only a few days ago.

And so, dear reader, I have come up with some wisdom bequeathed to me by Mama. I have dug deep in the memory bank and here are five ways that Mama said would guarantee us to stay svelte and slender without resorting to Jane Fonda's daily stretches or such contraptions like the counterpart to the "iron maiden" -- the stairmaster. (The very name sounds obscene.)

1. Eat only when standing up. Food consumed in this way contains very few calories and the few that do remain descend quickly to the bottom of your feet and quickly disappear.

2. Bread is a no-no. But if you crave a slice of bread, eat toast. Toast, you see, has no calories; they are all burned away in the toaster.

3. A large piece of chocolate cake containing 500 calories will contain but a fraction of that amount if consumed at three or four sittings -- or eatings. With food, unlike geometry, the whole is not at all equal to the sum of its parts.

4. Everyone knows that there is a direct correlation between weight and good humor. (This is not an ice-cream commercial), since somehow fat people laugh a lot and the skinnies are all solemn folk. So stop giggling and get serious. The pounds will roll away like water off a – you get the idea.

5. *And finally THINK THIN!* Keep your head up and your chins high (or is it your chins up and your head high?) and don't look down. Remember if God had wanted us all to be slim, He wouldn't have created calories or scales.

Sounds easy? It's sure-fire. If you have any doubts, ask the cheerful chubbies who have lost 46 pounds over the past several years – and have put back 53! And, remember, when all else fails, you can always thump your *tush* against the door post for a count of thirty each day and then, like Rosalind Russell, throw up your hands and give a *geshrai*, "The heck with it! Let it spread!"

A Girl Is Not A Woman and A Tushie Is Not A....

"The children today...they don't know how to speak correctly."

"The children today..." I waited because I knew that Mama had to complete the sentence and I didn't want to be rude and interrupt. There was really no point in stopping Mama in the midst of a thought. It would do me no good. She would just glare at me, then smile and then add, "I'm still talking...*Dahling*."

And this "*Dahling*" had an acerbic edge. So I waited. And after a two second pause, she added, "*Oy*." Now she was finished and the thought, as well as the sentence, had come to a conclusion.

"The children today..." I coaxed. And she gave another sigh like the burdens of the national debt, the homeless, and the problems of socialized medicine were all on her shoulders. "...they don't know how to speak correctly."

Aha, so now it was out and we could defer the problem of dealing with HMO's and the burden of taxation (the rich get richer and the poor pay taxes) off to another visit.

I returned one of Mama's Mona Lisa smiles to her, folded my hands in my lap and let her go on. She needed no additional encouragement.

"You listen on the television and the words they use. A *shandeh*. Even in Yiddish I wouldn't repeat some of those words, except maybe for *"tushie"* and only when I mean a grandchild's *tushie*, but never about a big person."

I explained as best I could that we are living in the modern era and that people express themselves differently, that the rules of propriety have changed, and that vocabulary, too, has undergone a different development.

I knew that I didn't convince her – in fact, I didn't convince myself, let alone this ninety-year-old woman of the world. So I simply asked, "Something special that you have in mind?"

"Have another slice of sponge cake. Eat...eat. It's not fattening. I cut down on the sugar and I used more egg whites than the yellow. Don't think I don't know what's good and what is bad. How can home-baked cake be bad?"

She was straying from the topic, but I complied and took a piece of cake, which was really quite good. I told her so. She was genuinely pleased. "You're easy to satisfy. I only wish I could bake like your Bubbie. She knew how to make sponge cake...mmmmnnnn."

And then after a pause, the story came out.

"Last week I was sitting in front of the house. I brought down my chair and I was with the girls near the empty lot so that the Super wouldn't chase us. Then, who should come to visit but Fat Rosie's granddaughter – the one with the glasses and the funny hair. She came by with a few friends and I heard her use a word that wasn't proper, especially for a girl."

I couldn't resist. "What word, Mama?" I tried, but lost.

"All she told me was, 'It wasn't *tushie*, believe-you-me.' So I told her so. You know I have a big mouth. I said, 'A girl should be careful what comes out of her mouth.' And she said, 'A girl! I'm twenty-three. I'm not a girl. I'm a woman.'

"Well, my teeth almost fell from my mouth and I had to explain that even some of the ladies who were sitting with us were still girls – Beatie Green was a girl even though she was past eighty, and her sister Mamie, too. Neither of them had ever been married. So they were girls."

A pause, so I prompted, "And then..."

Mama looked me straight in the eye, "And then she told me a thing or three. She said that I was confusing the word 'girl' with 'vir...virg...' I won't repeat to you, but she told me that she didn't know about Beatie or Mamie, but that she was certainly not a 'girl.'

I thought that Fat Rosie would have a heart attack, and Mamie had a coughing fit and got so red in the face that I thought she was having a conniption. I refrained from laughing and only said, "So?"

"So," Mama concluded, "so, you have to be correct when you speak. A girl is not a woman and a *tushie* is not a..."

She stopped in the middle, "I'm sure you get the idea. After all, you teach English in a college. Just tell the boys and girls that they should watch what comes out of their mouths. And tell the girls especially that they should take care...if you know what I mean."

I knew, but I believe in the words of our sages that "a fence around wisdom is silence."

So all I said was, "I'll take another piece of sponge cake to wash down the tea."

Jose Rubio Is Dead

"I'm not afraid of commas anymore."

Jose Rubio is dead. There was a brief, very brief, account on the radio news broadcast. On my way to the college, I turn on the news channel on the car radio so I can hear about the latest mugging and robberies in New York. And this day there was mention of a young male Hispanic, about thirty years old, who had shot his common-law wife and then turned the gun on himself.

After that brief report came the weather – cloudy and overcast with a chance of severe thunderstorms. There was the ten percent chance of a better day on the way.

Don't count on it.

I felt a knot in my stomach. I remembered that about ten years ago I had taught a young man – Jose Rubio. He was a student in my remedial English class. He had failed remedial writing three times and so this was his fourth try to "make it" so that he could enter the normal current of academic work.

I remember that he told me he would never be able to master the complexities of English sentences – with subjects and verbs, sentences swarming with participles and conjunctions, and peppered with apostrophes and semi-colons. Spelling seemed to follow no rules or punctuation that he was aware of.

But Jose had an open smile and seemed to respond to

25

my attempt to assure him that we would work together. In fact, he turned out to be a hard-working, dedicated student. He was always prompt and never missed a class – even on days when he came in with a hacking cough.

His writing began to improve, slowly, very slowly. At times, he seemed to want to shield me from disappointment, especially when I returned a composition to him filled with little red scratches and marginal notes instructing the writer to check the spelling of a word or to insert a better mark of punctuation.

Jose looked at the paper, smiled and told me, "Don't be sad, Dr. Leo. It's really my fault."

But I *was* sad, and so arranged for him to receive special tutoring in the writing lab. He appeared to do better with instruction given on a one-to-one basis and by the end of the semester – as they sing in *Fiddler* – "Miracle of Miracles" – he became a "passing" student.

A week before the final examination, on a theme supervised and graded by two professors who were supposed to be objective and uninvolved, Jose came to my office every day for an hour of tutoring. It was apparent that he enjoyed the personal relationship with me, coupled with the cup of tea and home-baked cookies.

"I'm not afraid of commas anymore," he told me, and it did seem that his smile was more relaxed, that he held his head a bit higher.

"Do you think I'll pass this time?" he asked me and I said, "You'll do fine, just fine." And he did. Both instructors who graded Jose's paper indicated that he could go on to college-level English.

Jose came to see me from time to time. Occasionally he came with a question about grammar or sentence structure, but I recognized that this was a thinly veiled subterfuge. He came for conversation.

I found out that he had no parents, no relatives. At holiday time, we even exchanged gifts because he told me that there was no one who would give him a gift, and perhaps even more important, he needed someone to give a present to.

Jose dropped out of college in the middle of a semester. He never completed his course requirements. He felt that he needed a full-time job "to keep going." He really wasn't academically oriented and I only said, "Good luck and keep in touch."

I saw Jose twice after he left school. The first time was to visit him in the hospital. He had called to tell me that he had to undergo some minor surgery, and I went to see him when he was recuperating.

The second time occurred completely by chance. I was driving out of a shopping mall, and Jose was standing near a Wells Fargo truck. I stopped my car and we exchanged a few pleasantries. But I was holding up traffic, and I was in a rush to get home, and I was tired, and so I concluded the conversation with the familiar cliche, "Keep in touch."

His voice sounded a bit more sincere than mine when he said, "I will, Dr. Leo. I will. I promise." Jose did not keep that promise.

I contacted the police and spent a half hour at the precinct, verifying what I already knew – Jose Rubio was dead. His last job was with Wells Fargo and his supervisor said he was a pleasant guy and a good worker. Reliable and dependable, but he kept to himself.

I taught Jose Rubio the use of the apostrophe and how to construct a complete sentence. But he needed more. A colleague told me that I shouldn't feel any responsibility. (The Jewish word is guilt.)

But for many years I have been lecturing on Jewish Literature and I know full well that it is written in the Talmud that if you save one man's life, it is as if you have preserved the world.

And now that Jose Rubio is dead, will the world be destroyed? I close my eyes and when I open them, the world is still there…but seen through a mist.

Bubbie — Tzedakah, Discipline, and Arms Designed for Hugs.

In halting English she said, "You come!"

When I was five years old, I learned a lesson that has remained with me for my entire life. So let's go back a little bit. (Little, ha!) It happened that Grandma (of course, we called her "Bubbie") lived with us. She was well advanced in years, and in those days you didn't talk about putting the elderly members of the family in a Senior Citizen's Residence. (Think we had even heard the phrase "senior citizen?")

All that I remember was that Bubbie did not speak English, that she was a wonderful baker and cook (what she could do with an onion, a carrot, a sweet potato, a— my mouth still waters), that her arms were designed for hugs and embraces, that she smelled warm and soft, and that I was the apple of her eye. We loved each other completely and I knew that as far as my Bubbie was concerned I could do no wrong. I could never do anything that was not absolutely perfect…one hundred per cent. Never. Until…

And so the story. Each week, on Friday, Bubbie baked the special Shabbos Challahs (That's Challahs with a "Ch" as in Chanukah. You know. Of course, you do.) And also sponge cake, honey cake, and cookies. (There goes the mouth watering again.) And then, hand-in-hand, we walked five blocks to the Hebrew Orphan Asylum on Clay Avenue in the Bronx. (In those days there was a Hebrew Orphan Asylum. And there was also a Bronx. See me after class, if you still don't understand.) She gave the delicacies to the Rebbe, a man of indeterminate age with a very determinate beard, and then she had a cup (actually a glass) of tea while I went into the yard and played with the children who lived in the home. This happened every week. Shabbos came every week and we went to the Hebrew Orphan Asylum each week.

Although I didn't particularly care for the time I spent with *those* children (they really weren't my friends), I somehow knew that this was my obligation, the cross (oops...) that I had to bear. But then came that Friday when I said, "No." I wasn't going to go with Bubbie. I preferred staying at home and playing with the little boy next door. So I said, "No."

For a minute there was a silence, a silence like the sound of angel voices. Bubbie looked at me and I looked at her. And then she spoke...in halting and difficult English, a language that did not come easily, "You come."

I turned to Mama and Papa to enlist possible allies. But Papa had already retreated to the bathroom, newspaper in hand, and locked the door. This could be a long siege. Mama who never argued with Bubbie— except maybe about whether to put an extra carrot in the chicken soup — started to defend my position. "Just this week...he's only a child...next week for sure... Bubbie didn't budge. Her eye was fixed on me and all she did was repeat, "You come." And I knew that I had lost.

I tried one last maneuver, one final effort. I held out a few coins that I had been saving to help defray the cost of some desired toy. "Take this," I offered. "Put it in the *tzedaka* (charity, in case you needed to know. But you didn't.) box." And then...and then there came a flood of words. Bubbie let me have it with all the strength she could muster, a tirade of English that I never knew she possessed, so many English words and a few choice Yiddish expressions thrown in as well. How could I be so selfish...to try to buy my way out of doing an act of kindness, doing a real mitzvah, being thoughtful of others, to offer a few pennies so that I could cut myself off from my own flesh...When she finished I took her hand, and once again, hand-in-hand, we walked without speaking, to Clay Avenue. The only time that this silence was broken was when Bubbie turned to me, and in a soft but firm accent said, "We do not speak of this again."

And we did not. And each week I went with Bubbie. And each week I played with the children when Bubbie had a glass-of tea and delivered the *Shabbos* breads and cakes. Bubbie continued to hug me and tell me little stories about life in the old country and cradle me in her arms until three years later when she died and all the hugs stopped.

But the lesson remained. I know that as long as there is a child in the world who needs someone to play with, a child who is alone, I should wish most fervently that there would be someone who could hold out a hand to a more fortunate youngster and say, "You come."

The Academy "Reward" for Making New Friends

*"The children need a father...not an
old Jewish Bubbie."*

"One thing," Tanta Pesha always said, "when
it comes to making friends, your Mama
gets the 'Academy Reward.'"

Now normally I would correct her and tell her
Academy 'Award.' But I knew she would only give me
one of those special Pesha smiles and say "Whatever."
I let her continue.

She did. "She's made a new friend. This young
Korean lady, or maybe she's Chinese, whatever, just
came over and lives on the ground floor with the three
little children. The oldest is not even in school yet, and
guess what?"

I didn't try to guess. With both Mama and Tanta
Pesha, it's better not to guess...believe me. I offered a
weak smile, just enough to encourage her to continue.

"And now they're in each other's apartments. All the
time. I could go on. But I've got so much to do. The
bathroom has to be cleaned and the ice box needs to be
defrosted. If I stay on the phone with you...like Fat
Rosie in 3C, nothing will get done. So better you
should come over and visit. Then I can tell you and you
can tell me." The telephone clicked.

And I called Mama. "I hear you have a new friend."

I heard Mama's laugh. "So Tanta Pesha has been telling you. Such a nice woman (I knew this did not refer to Pesha) with three such adorable children (this certainly was not Pesha) and the oldest is not even four. And their Mama lives all alone. Her husband went somewhere looking for work. So of course, I take care of the children while she goes out shopping."

"You baby-sit?" There was a note of incredulity in my voice. After all, Mama was close to ninety – and three small children...!

But Mama ignored the tone in my voice. "Someone has to help," she explained, letting me know that Nature abhors a vacuum and Mama was ready to fill the void. And then she told me, "It's hard for her. She doesn't speak a word of English – and the children too."

I surmised that that meant that the children knew no English. "So how do you get along?" I knew that Mama had no knowledge of Chinese or Korean.

"We talk. Easy. And I could go on, but I promised Mrs. Su that I would bring her lunch and I made a fresh noodle pudding with fruit and cottage cheese. Low fat – but she doesn't have to worry about calories – so skinny she is."

And so the weeks went by and the stories about Mama and the nice lady on the ground floor multiplied. Until one day, Tanta Pesha informed me that a change had taken place. "She moved away." (I knew that the "she" was not Mama, but the Korean Lady with the three small children.) "She went to join her husband. He found a good job."

I called Mama to find out how the change had affected her. "I hear that Mrs. Su has left."

Again came the little chuckle in her voice to let me know that Tanta Pesha was at it again. "Such a nice lady and such a good friend. But she's better off – the children need a father, not an old Jewish *Bubbie* – and now they speak some English and also (again a wry chuckle) a little Yiddish. It can't hurt."

I knew that Mama would miss her friend, the nice Korean Lady on the ground floor and I told Mama so. She was philosophic. "That's life, *Dahling*. Some come. Some go. And not Korean – *Vietnamese*. And I can't talk now. I have a potato *kugel* in the stove. The lady that moved in on the ground floor has a ten-month-old baby and I think she's already pregnant, and she has no time for lunch.

So I...I can't go on – it's too long a story. But Tanta Pesha will tell you all about it, I'm sure."

And she did.

Papa's Battle —
Checker Tournament vs. The Job

"This was only a game. A job was a job."

The game of checkers was Papa's great love. Perhaps "love" is not strong enough – passion might be better. Mama used to say, "If your Papa had to choose between me and his checkers, better not ask."

And so there is a mixed emotion when I remember the Great Checker Tournament. Every year there was a tournament to discover who the champion checker player would be. And THAT year the tournament was held in The Bronx, our own borough.

Of course, Papa entered. Who could have the slightest doubt? And he played and he played and he played. He competed against all challengers each week. When Sunday came, Papa would appear in St. James Park on Kingsbridge Road.

He came promptly at nine in the morning and competed. Mama would be there with a thermos of hot coffee and a few oranges cut into slices. The coffee was there in case he got thirsty. And the oranges…well he had to keep up his strength.

And all of us kids gathered about to watch and cheer him on. Of course the "him" referred to whomever your father or uncle or grandfather or even neighbor might be. In my case, there was little left to the imagination. It was Papa.

He just had to win. The winner would receive a gold medal, the runner up would receive a silver medal, and the rest would get …we didn't even entertain in our minds what the others might receive. There was a place on the wall in the foyer where Papa was going to hang the gold emblem of achievement.

That was all we thought about, dreamed about and – if I must reveal – prayed about. Oh God, I said each night before I went to bed, please…please… The prayer was not only for me – it was really for Papa.

The final match was to take place on June the eighteenth. Such an auspicious day! Not only was it Father's Day, but it was also Papa's birthday. And this was the day of the finals. Only two were left to compete. Papa couldn't lose. He had been up all night memorizing moves, studying interesting maneuvers.

I even asked God to intervene. Maybe his competitor could get sick. Not something serious, but just enough so that he wouldn't show up. Then Papa could win by default.

But the Powers-That-Be did not arrange things so easily. In fact, it was that Sunday that Papa had to go to work in the afternoon. He was a motion picture projectionist and that Sunday he had the early shift. He had to be at work at noon.

Mama kept assuring us that it was only one game and that it would be over well before noon – from her mouth to God's ears. But as the sages tell us: *Mann tracht und Gott lacht.* (The French say, *L'homme propose et Dieu dispose.*) We say, *Man plans and God…*You get the message…Why kick a dead horse?…So many proverbs in one story.

The game proceeded slowly and the hands of the clock moved rapidly. The two men were evenly matched. Papa was up against very stiff competition and then Mama said, "You have to go to work."

Papa pleaded, "Ten more minutes, maybe fifteen. I'll take a taxi." A taxi! No one in our family ever spent money on a taxi before. Wow!

It was up to the competitor to move. He took his time. "Move!" we yelled silently. "Papa has to go to work!." Mama pleaded... cajoled ...begged. This was only a game. A job was a job. It put food on the table. The depression motif still was part of her psyche. Papa looked at Mama. Their eyes met. His said, "You could call in and say I'm sick." Hers said... but I couldn't tell, because she was crying.

So you know the end of the story. That is – you know if you know about the depression, about the nightmare of unemployment, about the Jewish family mentality...   Papa forfeited the game. With head bowed, he left the table in the park and went to work.

So Papa got the silver medal and Mama displayed it on the wall in the foyer so that everyone who came into our home – every relative, every neighbor, every friend could see. And Mama would say with pride and love, "See – a silver medal." And once I heard Papa say under his breath...only once..."It could have been gold."

2. All In The Family

Making a Choice: Complain & Whine or Be Funny and Clever

"Maybe good things come in small packages, but so does poison. So watch out."

She was not quite eleven, but everyone said she was big for her age. And she was in the fifth grade at P.S. 2 in New York. The year was 1903. That's when it happened.

She was walking with a classmate down a flight of stairs leading from the third floor to the second floor, when a group of older boys came rushing down behind her. She was not fast enough to get out of the way and so she was pushed down the flight of steps onto the hard concrete landing below.

A teacher was summoned and the little girl was taken to the principal's office. They waited for several hours until someone was able to tell her mother. (There were no telephones available.) But by the time her mother came, the child was in severe pain and had to be taken to the neighborhood hospital. How she got there, she does not remember. A taxi was out of the question and there were no people with cars willing to drive her.

The doctors said she would need back surgery to correct the injuries. But there was no money available. Her mother did not speak English and her Papa had died several years ago, a victim of the pneumonia epidemic that had plagued New York City.

So the doctors, who had no time or patience with this Mama who spoke only a foreign tongue ("I think it's called Yiddish," one of the attendants remarked) gave the child a bottle of pills and some hurried instructions (including, "You're getting these free so you better take them and be grateful.") and sent the two home, warning them both that the kid better stay in bed for several weeks and not go back to school.

The child obeyed. She stayed in bed and took all the pills. And she cried. She missed her friends. She missed school. And she even missed helping take care of her little brother. She even wished she could help clean the house. But she couldn't. Finally she was able to walk again, but she was stooped over. And when she went back to the doctor (the same hospital, but another doctor) she was told that she had a severe spinal curvature, that she would probably never grow any more, and that she would never be able to have children.

Of the three, which was the worse news? Her Mama cried. And when she went back to school, she was called a "hunchback." She was called clumsy and the teacher told her to sit in the back of the room so as not to distract the other children.

It was then that she decided she had a choice. She could spend her life complaining and whining and saying that life isn't fair. (In later years, one of her favorite expressions was, "Laugh and the world laughs with you; cry and you better get a lot of tissues.")

Or she could stand as straight as she could, pull herself up to her four feet, nine inches, and be as funny and as clever as possible. ("You better be careful," she told her teasing and taunting classmates, "Maybe good things come in small packages, but so does poison. So watch out.")

And the little girl went on and finished grammar school and worked as a salesperson, and earned money and helped support her brother through high school and her widowed Mama. And she helped with the cleaning and the household chores. And even though she never grew any more than she was at eleven, she used to say, "Thank God, I was tall for my age, even though I'm short for my age now."

And one day she even met a young man who was a trolley car conductor and who said he didn't care that she came only up to his *pupik*; and who could see beyond the twisted back; and who said that when she smiled, even when it was raining, the sun was out.

And so the two of them were married and moved to an apartment big enough to include the widowed mother. And they lived together for fifty years and the little girl, who had become a woman, always said, "God was so good to me. I am so grateful!"

And that little eleven year old girl who was pushed down a flight of steps in P.S.2 and who never grew any more and who was told by the doctor in the Big Hospital that children would never be part of her life – that little girl became My Mother and made certain that I had a brother as well.

So as Tanta Pesha so often said, "So go listen to doctors! Like you think they know everything! 'Ha!' That's what I say."

And that's what I say too!

Wishing for More Display of Love

"I never heard them speak to each other of love."

We were not the Walton Family. That's for starters. Mama and Papa were not the prototypes for Jeanette MacDonald and Nelson Eddy or Myrna Loy and William Powell. (Now if you don't know those names, see me after class and I will explain.)

The truth is that, even though there were loads of hugs for the children, there just wasn't a lot of open affection between Mama and Papa. No frequent hugging or kissing or even holding hands – in public that is. And somehow I think I would have liked to see more display of "love."

And yet…(You know there is always an 'and yet.')

Papa never went beyond the sixth grade in elementary school. As soon as he reached his teen years, he had to work. All his siblings (there were nine of them) followed this pattern I am told. But he managed to get jobs and bring home a few dollars to help out his family. Eventually he became a street car conductor and then he met Mama who was working as a salesperson (see, I used the politically correct word) and they were married.

For Mama, she couldn't believe her good fortune. She used to tell me, "He was slim with dark, wavy hair, and tall." (Actually he was 5' 7" but to Mama, who was stooped over and only 4' 9" – that was tall!)

And when she told him that she might not be able to

"give him children," he simply said, "So we'll adopt." This was a real *mensch*. And then Mama would add, "And believe me, there wasn't a line-up of eligible young men waiting to grab me." But they fooled everyone and became parents…not once, but twice.

And Papa went on to become an electrician and then a motion picture projectionist. And Mama said, "Such hands that man has. And smart too – even without a diploma. There's nothing he doesn't know!" For example, Mama never changed a light bulb. When the bulb needed to be replaced, no one was allowed to go near it. "Wait until your Father comes home," we were admonished. And indeed when Papa came home from work, and after he had his dinner and a glass of tea with a slice of lemon, then he was asked to change the bulb.

And Mama exclaimed, "Look how easy he does it!" And the children were summoned to see the miracle that had occurred. "Look at that!" Mama exclaimed. "One-two-three, Papa changed the bulb and now we have better light. In a million years I could not have done it." And Papa blushed and Mama *kvelled* with pride. "That man knows everything!"

And when it was raining, Mama left the house, even at midnight or later – an umbrella in hand – to wait for Papa by the subway station when he came home after the night shift, so that he shouldn't get wet. And the next morning when Papa scolded Mama, "In the middle of the night I don't want you should wait for me with an umbrella. It's only four blocks and I won't melt."

But Mama only told him, "So what else do I have to do? And who else do I have to run for? Maybe the mailman or the milkman? No such big deal."

And if Papa had a cold, she would be sure to bring him a thermos of hot tea and a few *ruggelach* to keep up his strength. And even though he said it wasn't necessary, she told him in no uncertain terms that he needed liquids and there was also a container of orange juice mixed with grapefruit juice, all fresh squeezed, because the vitamins were good for him and coffee he doesn't need – the tea is better – and "finish all the juice with the pulp too because that's where the vitamins are."

And when Mama had saved a little extra in the chipped sugar bowl, she bought Papa a white shirt or a tie or new socks for a special occasion. And when he told her, "Better you can buy a new dress for yourself," she only laughed and said, "I need more to keep the closet company? And besides, a man has to look presentable when he goes to work. You want everyone to think you're a *shlumper* and that I don't take care of you so the neighbors will have something to gossip about?" And you couldn't argue with that.

So they were not the Waltons and we were not the Brady Bunch. But we managed. And even though I never heard them speak to each other of love, (oh how I wish I could have heard that!) still, I remember what the Kotzker Rebbe said – that the silent prayer speaks the loudest of all.

And I wouldn't want to contradict Mama or Papa or especially the Kotzker Rebbe. Would you?

Prizes, Charity, and A Trip To Church

And the second prize was ... a ham!

Mama did not go to church. Let me explain this sentence. I mean that Mama in all her more than ninety-five years did not enter a church – not on a regular basis (which I am sure you understand) – or even on an infrequent basis.

This is not to be taken that Mama was a racist (Perish forbid!) or that she bore any ill feeling to those of a different religious persuasion. It was just... well... just... or better yet, as Mama herself would have said if asked, "I never really had the occasion."

And yet when she was past eighty-five, a widow living alone in The Bronx, Mama entered a church. And so the story.

But first we must establish that Mama was not a gambler. She didn't play bingo and Atlantic City would never have honored her with her picture among the "High Rollers." But she could never refuse a request to give a few coins to help in some philanthropic or charitable enterprise. In her foyer, in the little apartment that she managed, there was a table, and on that table were ever so many slips of paper testifying that Mama had bought a raffle or contributed to some cause.

When I asked her about the latest papers, she told

me, "I think that's cancer, or arthritis, or MS (you shouldn't know from that – it's a terrible disease) the lady told me, so I gave a dollar."

And when I continued to probe, she continued as well. "And that's for the Girl Scouts – such a cute child came, sweet little girl – I think she lives on the fifth floor. How could I say 'no?' And this one, it's for something with cardia or vasquez or something that sounds terrible. Must be a disease. No? May God protect us from such sicknesses! And this last one, let me remember..."

I waited patiently while the little gray cells in the cerebrum began to come together, and then finally the little light went on and she continued, "Oh this last one, now I remember, it's from the neighborhood Center. You know – where the old people go, the ones that don't have anything to do and live with their children, poor things. This is a raffle to help the homeless."

Somehow the elderly living with their children and the homeless merged into one entity. I had lost track and couldn't follow and I wanted to change the subject, but Mama was persistent. That, she was. "Who knows – maybe I'll win yet. The first prize is a trip to Disney World. Not that I need such a trip, but I'll give it to you."

She was magnanimous, sharing this un-won prize with me. So what could I do, but look into that smiling face and say, "Thank you."

So now imagine my surprise when a few weeks later the telephone rang and Mama's excited voice on the other end informed me that I should start to pack my valise. I was off to Disney World with the whole family.

"You'll send me a post card. Don't buy me any souvenirs. *Chachkes* I don't need. More to dust."

I couldn't believe the call. There must have been some mix-up, some confusion.

There was. Mama did not win the first prize. She

was a winner, however. The second prize. And the second prize was a... HAM! Honest to Tanta Pesha! A ham, and they were going to deliver it that afternoon. Poor Mama. A ham was one of those most forbidden foods and even to put it into her refrigerator, if indeed it fit, next to the blintzes made with no-fat cottage cheese, was out of the question.

But for every problem there is a solution. So Mama was prepared for the delivery of the second prize. She put on her *Shabbos* dress and even wore a hat and a new – well almost new, but certainly not so old – sweater, and when the young man brought the ham ("I gave him a quarter tip. After all...") she had him place it in her shopping cart and off she went.

You guessed it... to church. She walked in *shlepping* the cart behind her and found the priest, Father Curran. She was bringing him a gift for the poor.

"You must know some non-Jewish homeless or poor," she told him. "Here, this is for them. You take care of it. Yes?"

And she related the whole story complete with cancer and MS and Girl Scouts and cardia-vasquez (a sickness?) and he listened patiently and then he thanked her for her generosity.

And as she left, shopping cart in tow, Father Curran said, "And I will say a prayer for you this Sunday."

And Mama called to the good Father, "And I'll say one for you."

And she did.

Grandkids & Havdallah Services

"So go. It's a mitzvah. Never refuse a child."

The high pitched voice at the other end of the wire was unmistakable. "Grandpa, do you know who this is?"

I decided to play the game, "The President of the United States? Now what do you want? I'm a bit tired. And this is still the Sabbath so I'm not going to talk business with you."

There came a laugh from the other, un-presidential end. I was being rewarded by that seven year old chuckle. "Oh Grandpa, I'm not the President."

I didn't hesitate for a moment before answering, "Well, you could have fooled me." And so the voice continued, "Micah and I want to know something."

I was not finished with my game, "Micah?" I questioned, "Is that the new Secretary of State?" Of course, I knew full well that this was the oldest sibling in the four child family, but after all, you can't blame a grandfather for trying. But then again, even great comedy has its limits.

"So what do you need to know?" I asked as I removed my socks and stretched out on the couch. It had been one of those days and every bone and sinew let me know how good it would be just to take ten minutes or more to nap – and as Walt Whitman so ably put it, "to loaf and invite your soul." And believe you me this soul needed quite a bit of inviting.

But man proposes and the seven-year-old disposes as he said, "So Grandpa, will you take Micah and me to *shul* for *havdalah* services?"

Now I must admit that this was not on my agenda for this Saturday evening. Now don't misunderstand me. I happen to love this final service of the Shabbat when we bid farewell to the *Sabbath Queen*, but most of the time (and don't ask me to clarify "most") we conduct this service at home when I can wear comfortable (what my wife calls, the "ratty") slippers.

But how can one refuse this request (plea? command? offer?) from a grandchild? I could hear Mama telling me (or was it my Bubbie? Or maybe Tanta Pesha? Or probably all three in unison like a Greek chorus. Now there's a mixed metaphor if I ever heard one!) "So go, it's a mitzvah. And never refuse a child. Especially for something like this."

So we went. I had scarcely had time to remove my ratty slippers and put on my *shul* shoes (say that three times fast and see what happens. Aha!) when the "boys" appeared at the door, with *yarmulkes* on their *keppies* and off we went.

When we entered, Rabbi Krauss' face (a real cherubic *ponim)* took on an even more angelic smile and the twinkle in his eyes radiated affection as he greeted us. (Or as Tanta Pesha would say, "like you were the Queen of England – only better. And Jewish.") and we joined him in chanting the ancient melodies as we bid farewell to the departing Sabbath Presence.

And then wonder of wonders, miracle of miracles (now that would make good lyrics to a song!), he summoned Ari and Micah to the front of the congregation. And Ari held the braided candle (Hold it high, advised David, and you'll get a tall bride) and Micah conducted the service. And then the candle was lit, the spice box passed around, the wine was sipped (don't correct me on the order), the candle extinguished, and the whole group burst into the melody summoning Elijah the Prophet and urging him to appear.

And then...and then...best of all...since this was the first time that Micah had conducted a Havdalah service, everyone pronounced the prayer *She-heh-che-yanu*, giving thanks for allowing us to rejoice at this most special of occasions.

There was the scent of the spices and the flickering of the flames and aroma of sweet wine. There was the joy of the song and for a minute I thought that the Rabbi heard a noise at the door – and he turned around and so did I – and his eye caught mine, but we didn't exchange a word. After all, the departure of the Sabbath Queen and the summoning of the good Prophet Elijah, were just parts of our traditional folklore and not reality.

And besides, when I turned to the door there were tears in my eyes. Could I be coming down with a cold? Or was it... You fill in the rest.

Signs, Righteous Gentiles, and Chocolate

"I had warned her about good manners and proper decorum because this was a very important person."

Now as long as I can remember I always believed in signs. If the sign said "Stop" – I halted and waited. If the sign on the door read "Entrance" – that was where I went in. And of course, I left by the door marked "Exit."

Do you remember the story that P.T. Barnum used to tell? He put up a sign marked "This way to the Egress" and all the people proceeded obediently to view the rare animal that was being exhibited, only to discover that they had exited to the outside of the tent. I suppose that I would easily have been one of those.

Now one day, a sign appeared on the bulletin board of the college where I teach. In bold print it told us to "Take your child to work." In smaller letters (I had to move closer to read) the author of the sign pointed out the value of exposing our children to the "world of work."

It seemed like a fairly good idea so I decided to approach five-year-old Tamar, a delicious blond hair, smiley face, *shtick nachas* (You think that I'm prejudiced in my description? Not a bit. I'm only doing what grandfathers throughout the ages have done. It's tradition. Now I'm sounding like Tevye.) with the suggestion that she might like to come with me to college.

Her eyes lit up and the lips formed the affirmative and off we went skipping kindergarten, grade school, middle school, high school...

Our first stop was the library where we looked at all the stacks of books and Tamar opened up one to me that was on a table and spent some time turning the pages. The research librarian observed her for a minute and then in a delightfully solemn voice asked her if she found the book to be interesting. She didn't hesitate for a second before offering her critique, "Too many words and not enough pictures."

Enough intellectual stimulation, we (We? Ha!) decided. So we followed the sign which led us to the school cafeteria. This was more like it. We walked up and down the aisles as I pointed out the nutritional value of vegetables ("Doesn't that broccoli look good? Well how about the carrots and potatoes?") and the salad bar ("Everything looks so fresh. No, that's the color of the cabbage. It's not fake.").

And then Tamar turned aside, avoiding all my excellent suggestions for a highly nutritious snack and pointed to the frozen yogurt machine. "That's what I want," she declared with an emphasis that I had heard before. "You push the handle down and wow!"

So down went the handle and (wow!) out came the yogurt. Until I saw the biblical admonition of the cup, which had begun to run over and we stopped.

Next came the choice of toppings. I wanted the chocolate chips and she wanted the rainbow sprinkles, so we compromised with the sprinkles and, armed with two plastic spoons and a plastic bowl that was certainly not drip proof, we grabbed a handful of paper napkins and chose a table near the window where we made short work of the yogurt.

So time marches on and we followed in its footsteps. But there was one more sign – "Office of the Dean." And Tamar decided that this might be an interesting way to end our visit. So after I had warned her about good manners and proper decorum because this was a very important person, we entered. All the admonitions were wasted effort. I should have known better. For Tamar, it was love at first sight as soon as she saw the gentle smile and the sparkling eyes behind the spectacles, the warm voice that did not patronize and had the slightest of accents to betray its Dutch origin, and when he offered to share his hoard of chocolates with her… well I could easily have disappeared and no one would have noticed. Even a grandfather can not compete with some people. For our tradition tells us that the world exists because of thirty-six righteous individuals and I am certain in my heart of hearts that this Dean, who has devoted his professional life to seeing to it that our young people never forget the horror of the Shoah – the Holocaust Experience – this man who embodies what is the finest in the Christian tradition (and I suppose in the Jewish tradition as well), must be one of thirty-six, a real *lamed vovnik*.

And hours later after we had arrived home and I discovered that the brown spot on Tamar's overalls was the remainder of some melted chocolate ("I wanted to save it for later.") and I asked Tamar what she liked best of the day, there was no contest. And even when she said, "And you know I had never seen a 'dean' before!" I had to add, "Certainly not like this one."

And who cares if the stain doesn't quite come out. It's the memories that count.

Papa & Picket Duty

"It wouldn't be half bad if we could pick our signs."

Several times a year Papa came home from his Union meeting with an assignment. When Mama asked him what happened at the meeting, he told her that it was his time for "pick-a-duty." I never quite understood what kind of duty was available and how he decided to choose or "pick" the one that he did. But life was like that. Seven-year-olds were not obliged to understand the ways of the adult world.

"What duty did you pick?" I asked. And then I was told that Papa had to spend a week with a "sandwich board" and march up and down in front of a movie theater. The board that he carried was to inform all those who passed by that the Union had a grievance against the management of the theater and all good people should pass by, not purchase tickets, and certainly not even think of entering the theater – Even if there was a special cartoon or a serial that would be showing.

The rules were simple. You carried the board and you walked back and forth. You could not stand still. That was against the rules and if someone – anyone – looked as if he or she might consider purchasing a ticket, you stared, in fact, you glowered at the almost-culprit.

Talking was against the rules. But a good stare was

worth a thousand words. (So maybe a hundred. I exaggerate.) The stare informed the near-purchaser that entering this theater would be taking bread from our table, depriving Papa of a livelihood, and making Mama worry more than she needed to. This was the look that was the forerunner of "Jewish Guilt."

It wasn't until many years later when I reached adolescence and high school that I learned that "Pick-a-duty" was really Picket duty and that Papa had no option in choosing how he wanted to spend his spare time.

The sign that Papa carried informed all that the theater management was unfair to the workers, that the bosses were not nice people, and that the laborers all wanted to earn an honest living under union guidance.

But as a seven year old, I thought that if I had my way, I would carry a sign telling the world of all the people I loved. And even now that I am a wee bit more than seven (I heard that laugh!) I should happily volunteer for pick-a-duty if I could proclaim to the passers by that I am grateful for so many people who add joy to my life. And now I mean those outside the family because everyone knows that I adore them.

I should rather announce that I am indebted to Marylou, the lady who serves as a cashier when I get my morning coffee and who starts my day with a smile.

And then there's the ticket taker at the Margate Bridge, who always asks me if I had a good day and seems genuinely delighted when I respond that my day was simply great.

And I should not like to overlook the fantastic librarian who tells me about the latest book or tape that arrived and who doesn't make me feel like a pariah when I apologetically admit that I am "two days overdue."

And there's Alex who fixed my computer and Scott who managed to get my clock to chime on the hour and the waitress who understands that I prefer not to have ice in my water and that my vegetables should be steamed without butter or oil, and the wonderful ladies in the synagogue who inform me that they just finished reading my latest "Chalkdust" column and say some good things, and the gentleman who smiles when I appear at evening minyan and remarks so that all can hear, "Here comes the kid." That guy earns extra brownie points in my book and gets bold print on my sign.

So you get the idea. Picket duty or 'pick-a-duty" (whatever) wouldn't be half bad if we could all invent our signs. So enough from me already. Here's a magic marker. Now you get the oak tag and write your own sign. I can hardly wait to read it.

A Visit To Mama Must Entail Food

"It would be un-Jewish and inappropriate ...
to say the least."

A visit from a grandchild was always a big event. Certainly to Mama, living alone in a one bedroom apartment in The Bronx, it was. So it was no surprise to me when I got a telephone call and I immediately recognized the familiar voice.

"Hello, Mama," I said.

"It's me, *Dahling*," she said. (And even when I answered that I knew who the – "me" was, she did not hesitate to inform me. "It's ME – Mama." So all I could say was "Oh." I didn't dare tell her that I thought it might be Princess Diana, because that would have brought on a fifteen minute rejoinder.)

And so Mama informed me what I already knew. My sixteen-year-old, Steven – whom she always called *Stevele* or *Tattele...* or *shayne ponim* or whatever – would be coming by the following day. I already knew, but I feigned surprise and even added, "How nice!"

But there was a problem. With Mama there was always a problem. Every visit entailed some food. How could someone come to visit and you not serve even a piece of fruit and a piece of cake. It would be un-Jewish and inhospitable to say the least. A growing child needs food to keep him going, I was told. And there was no arguing with that bit of medical philosophy.

56

So Mama had gone to the bakery and bought a piece of strawberry cheesecake. So fresh, you could tell by just looking at it.

And to my next "How nice," there came the problem. Mama informed me (as if I didn't know) that she did not know how to keep temptation away from her palate. The mere presence of the cheesecake made her salivate, and now she had to keep that delicacy in her home for almost twenty-four hours...intact.

How could she prevent herself from not nibbling away at this festive offering. It would lie-in-wait in her refrigerator, calling her name.

Ever since the serpent tempted Eve...oh you already know about that one. But at least Eve could be forgiven. After all, she had no Mother to guide her. And all Mama had was ME. So I had to come up with an answer – a plan to keep Mama from devouring the cake.

And so my plan. It was brilliant. I told Mama to "psyche" herself, to tell herself over and over, that the cake in the refrigerator was "untouchable" – beyond the pale.

How could she do that? Easy. All she had to do was convince herself that bacon grease had fallen upon the cheesecake, rendering it *trayfe* – not kosher – and hence something that an observant Jewish lady would never eat.

That was the plan and we both agreed that it would work. I even called Mama an hour later just to discover if all was working according to our agreement. "No problem," I was told. And so I slept with a clear conscience that night.

No problem, did I say? Well, not until the next day when Son Stevie (or *Stevele*...whatever) came back from visiting Grandma.

"Everything was great," he said. "We had a great visit. I even ate two peaches and an apple and had a glass of 'skinny-milk' (Mama's term for skim milk) and a fig Newman." (You caught that one).

"And the cheese cake?" I asked.

"Cheese cake? No, no cake just the cookie."

I was on the phone, waiting for an explanation. What could have gone wrong with the perfect plan? And then I was told.

"You see," Mama explained in her perfect logic, "I told myself not to touch the cake because bacon grease was on it. And that was good until right before I went to sleep and was watching the television to find out if tomorrow would be nice. And so I opened the ice box (it was always an *ice box*) just for a *nosh* and I said to myself, 'Lena, don't touch the cake. It's got bacon grease on it.' – just like you told me. But then I thought. What's the matter with me? How could bacon grease get into my ice box. Impossible. So I ate the cake. Delicious. So fresh."

And I wondered if there was just a tinge of remorse in her voice. I'd like to say that there was, but to tell the truth…

Well who needs the truth? The fig Newmans were good. Maybe not so good as cheese cake, but they were served with a happy and well contented heart. And after all, isn't that what really matters?

Growing Things ...
Like Plants & Children

"You've got to speak to them."

Growing up in The Bronx, not far from the Grand Concourse, we kids knew that if we wanted to see trees and grass, we had to walk the seven or eight or ten blocks to either Echo Park or Claremont Park. And then there were signs that warned us "Keep Off The Grass."

We were told in advance that we could look but not touch, that we had to listen to the Parky. The Parky was the man with a long stick with a sharp nail at the end. His role in life was to keep the park clean. And hence the stick with the nail. Should a piece of litter fall on the ground, it would quickly be snapped up and deposited in the large sack he carried.

Somehow I got the ominous feeling that the large stick and the pointy nail might well snap up a disobedient child, so I kept my distance. And the familiar cry from my friends of "Look out, there comes the Parky!" served as a warning to all of us.

So I remember how happy I was when one day Tanta Pesha came by with a gift. It wasn't anyone's birthday or a special occasion, just a day. And there in her hands was a snake plant. (I've since learned from a dear friend, a modern-day Tanta Pesha, that the real name for the plant is Sanseveria, although there are those who call it "mother-in-law's tongue." But that's a sermon for another week.)

"It's good that the children have something to take care of, to watch over and to see grow," she told Mama and Papa. And we pleaded, hoping that we could keep the plant. Even Bubbie was excited, so there was no objection and the plant stayed.

We watered it and washed the leaves, and in the hot days of summer, the plant was given an "airing." It was placed on the fire escape outside the living room window. Actually we were not the only family who took care of our plants this way. We were on the third floor, but up and down, all the fire escapes had plants during the summer months. (God forbid that there should be a fire!)

The plant thrived under the ministration of all the kids (and even adults) and we even made cuttings and gave them as gifts to the super, to the teacher, to the mailman – to all who were our helpers. I once wondered whether the Parky might deserve a cutting, but this noble thought soon vanished when he chastised a friend for letting his ball roll on the fringe of the grass lawn. After all, one needn't be too generous.

Many years have passed. The grandchildren don't know what a Parky is. When they come to a grass lawn in a park-like area they feel free to roll or jump or even picnic. They have become used to trees and shrubs and grass and growing things. Warning signs, except when a lawn has been newly seeded, have ceased to be commonplace.

Of course, we tell them not to litter, but there are no long sticks with pointy nails to act as a deterrent. And, even better, our houses are filled with plants. We derive a good deal of pleasure from watching the green leaves sprout, the buds appear and the plants thrive.

And even my daughter, whose husband claims she has a "brown thumb" and tells me that if you want to have a plant go to its demise – leave it in her house for a week and proof at the end of the week – *geshstorben*, dead, finished...but now, even she has developed a special nurturing quality (perhaps after four children and one husband, it's a *sine qua non* for survival) and her little begonia is blossoming and her ficus is ficussing and her aloe is – enough already – you've got the message.

Which brings me to the finale... and the sermon is almost over and the *oneg* is about to begin. A few weeks ago this modern Tanta Pesha, the one who knows that a snake plant is really a sanseveria, came by and gave my four-year-old granddaughter a lesson in caring for plants, how to pinch back, how to prune and how to remove the dead leaves. I thought this was very courageous of her – to instruct a four-year-old in such specialized and intricate matters, until I realized that those were my plants that she was practicing on and using as specimens.

But Tamar, that's the four-year-old, listened most attentively and seemed to absorb all the good bits of instruction. Indeed a few weeks later Tamar was playing with her friends from down the road. They had their favorite dolls in their hands and I began to eavesdrop. (So now you know I'm a "listener.")

With maternal grace, that only a four-year-old girl is capable of, she hugged her baby doll in her arms and told her friends, "They need a lot of care. You have to clean them and feed them and give them water to drink. But even more important they need to be loved and spoken to. That's the only way for them to grow and be strong and healthy."

Was she talking about the care of plants or the nurturing of children? A flood of memories crowded my brain. There was The Bronx and the Parky and the snake plant and Tanta Pesha and Bubbie and the fire escape and the children – the ones who needed to be cared for and to have a growing thing to take care of. And so I wondered if Tamar meant plants or children and if, after all, was it important what she meant.

Better not to ask, I decided. Eavesdroppers should not interfere or interrupt. Her advice was – when all is said and done – sound advice for all growing things, whether they had stems or toes – or both. End of message.

The "Emes" —
The Truth vs. Superstition

"Now that you gotta do, or otherwise you're liable to get a k'nine a hara."

A few of the neighbors had dropped by. "So if you're not so busy, you'll come by and have some tea and cake and a little something," was the way that Tanta Pesha had approached the "girls" in her building.

And even when one or two offered a mock semi-hesitation, she had added, "So what else do you have that's so important. So you won't watch the talk show where all the *meshugenas* come together to talk about how their *zaydies* did such terrible things to them and that's why today they put on so much weight. Big deal. You'll come and sit and have a *nosh* and a little conversation. Better that you should be with real people than to sit by yourself like a mummy glued to the television set."

And so they came and had a little conversation – which in reality meant that Pesha did the talking and they did the listening – sipping tea and nodding approval.

Suddenly – in the midst of one of Tanta Pesha's asides, telling me, "Oh your Bubbie – she should rest in peace – could bake a honey cake like it melted before it reached your mouth," – suddenly Fat Rosie from 3-C sneezed.

"You see," said Tanta Pesha, "you sneezed on the truth. I'm not lying." Again Pesha continued extolling someone's baking and again a sneeze.

"The truth!" the good Pesha called out. "I never lie – not like those politicians or that one that got buried in the wrong place and they had to dig him up. *Vay iz mir!* Such a liar! But I'm no politician and I tell the *emes* – the truth – and Rosie proved it by sneezing."

"That's a superstition, Pesha," called out Gertie From The Top Floor, the one who has the granddaughter in the out-of-town college where the boys sleep in the same place with the girls – only not in the same room – but you never know.

"Superstition?" replied Pesha with a voice between an exclamation and a question. "Like breaking a mirror or going under a ladder? This is no superstition. Unless you call a superstition putting a red *bendel* on a baby when you first take him out for an airing."

Feigel joined in. "You're right, Pesha. Now that you gotta do, otherwise you're liable to get a *k'nine a hara*, you know…" and this she said in a half whisper, "…*the evil eye. Pu, pu, pu.*"

"I remember that my cousin Flossie – the fat one with the hips – she had such a beautiful baby, but she didn't listen. No red *bendel*. And everyone looked at the child and said how beautiful and how smart, and would you know…they gave a *k'nine a hara* and the next week…the colic. All night she was up with the child. So you see, *that* was no superstition."

Everyone, except for Gertie, clucked their tongues in assent.

But Tanta Pesha refused to be outdone. "Soon you'll be saying that when someone sews a button on you and you're wearing the jacket or the coat or the dress, you should chew on a piece of thread. Soon you'll be saying that *that's* a superstition. Ha!"

"No," Mamie agreed. "*That*, you gotta do – like throwing salt over your shoulder or like knowing that if you drop a fork, you'll get a letter. Now *that* happens. I know."

"Or like bringing bread and salt into a new apartment when you first move in," contributed Feigel, "or even before you move in. *That's* just common sense. Certainly you know that when you leave a *shiva* house, you walk out with your right foot first. No?"

Pesha smiled happily, "No? Yes! Of course. Not a superstition. A fact. A proven fact."

Someone sneezed again, and before a tissue could be offered, Tanta Pesha called out, "You see. It's the truth – the truth. She sneezed on the truth. Not a superstition at all.

And believe you me, I'm not one bit superstitious. Thank God for that. God forbid that *I* should be superstitious."

And with that she knocked on wood three times.

Dressing For An Affair

"You call that a dress? Pheh, pheh."

The phone rang. The voice on the line was unmistakable. "Hello..." I responded within a heartbeat. "Hello, Mama."

Again the familiar voice, "Hello. This is Mama."

Now I could have continued the game and said, "I know." But I've been at this dialogue too long, so all I responded was, "Oh. And what's new?"

"So what should be new? Thanks God, I'm talking and you're listening." And then after a brief, very brief pause, the shoe dropped. In slow but measured cadences I was informed by Mama, "Your Tanta Pesha is having an affair."

I was stunned and blurted out, "Tanta Pesha...an affair?... how is it?... can you be sure?...that's impossible..."

Mama was not at all perturbed by my stammering. She simply continued. "A wedding. (She had me. I had fallen hook, line and...enough.) You hear me – a wedding – from her Cousin Pearlie.

"You remember Pearlie With The Hair. It's her daughter, the one with the eyes. She's getting, married to a boy from up-state somewhere, maybe Yonkers, who knows?

"But at her age and with those eyes you can't be picky. And after the last time when she went with the boy from Brooklyn and got lost on the subway and he

66

never held down a job. *Oy* what a story!"

I was lost. I don't think I had yet recovered from the first announcement of Pesha and her Affair. All I could say was, "So, Mama, good. But what or where do *I* fit in?"

Another pause and then, *"Dahling,* she needs a new dress."

I wasn't sure if we were talking about Pesha or Pearlie's daughter, the one with the eyes, but I somehow opted for Pesha and I was right.

"Now you know, *Dahling,* Pesha would never ask, but if you could volunteer, maybe you could drive her to a department store. I know she wouldn't refuse you, she sort of hinted." Now I know that the Army taught everyone that the first rule was Never Volunteer. And driving Tanta to a department store to buy a dress was three steps worse than going to have root canal done without benefits of novocaine. But they did not know Pesha and the endodontist was not acquainted with Mama. So what could I do? I called Pesha and arranged, after much "I don't want to put you out. I know how busy you are. Still..."

The Department Store was worse than we expected. There were racks of dresses in half sizes, but each one drew negative comments from Tanta Pesha.

"That one is for a young person. A kid. A teeny bopper."

"That one makes me look too old."

"Beads, who needs beads? A simple dress is what I want."

"Purple – for me no. Yellow makes me look sallow – like I died and they forgot to bury me."

"Too long – I'll have to shorten. Too short – everyone has to see my legs."

And finally the *coup de grace*, the comment to end all comments – "A dress, You call that a dress? *Pheh, pheh* – a *shmateh* and look at the price. I would have to have my head examined to throw away good money on such flimsy material. And what do I need a dress for? I have such nice clothing in my closet that I never wear.

But thank you for insisting that we come. Better I should have stayed at home and cleaned out the ice box instead of *shlepping* all the way to look at such rags."

And so we returned home. Tanta Pesha to hers and I to mine. And weeks later Tanta Pesha had her affair. She wore her blue suit with the buttons. And everyone told her how well she looked, that the suit made her look so slim (no comment from me) and that after all, what did it matter Pearlie's daughter with the eyes wouldn't have noticed if she (Tanta Pesha, that is) came dressed in a potato sack.

So all's well. And even though we never got a new dress (again, Tanta Pesha, that is), the story has a happy ending and as Mama pointed out, I did a *mitzvah*, and one day I'll get my reward.

And let me tell you – we can all use as many brownie points as we can earn. Believe you me.

Mama's Sugar Bowl Philosophy

"Let Mrs. Rockefeller worry about where to buy a fur coat."

I shall never forget that great moment in Yiddish theater when in re-enacting Shakespeare's *King Lear* (or as the playbill announced *Der Koenig Lear*, Lear asks each of his daughters (of course, he asked in Yiddish, what else?) to profess in words their love and devotion. And both those miseries (or as Mama would call them *chaleryas*... she wouldn't use the "B" word even if she thought it) spoke in glowing and false hyperbole of their love.

But sweet, gentle Cordelia (played by sweet, gentle Celia Adler of blessed memory) simply said, *"Gornisht"* "Nothing."

And then came the response from that irascible old curmudgeon (I've never before used that word in writing), *"Fun gornisht kumt gornisht."* I suppose that you could translate that into, *"Nothing comes from nothing,"* but...

I remember that I was told that the Stage Manager at the Second Avenue Yiddish Theater once remarked after watching King Lear in Yiddish, "Such a good play! They should translate it into English!"

So that brings me to the memory. As kids we were told by those far older and wiser than we, that 'you get nothing for nothing.' In life you had to pay your way. Fat Rosie From Apartment 3-C always spoke of the

"Almighty Dollar" and Gussie With The Hair responded that, "With money you get honey."

This was the kind of pragmatism that we learned in the street.

And at home there was a corresponding philosophy and it was centered in Mama's famous sugar bowl, the one with the chip. Here is where Mama kept spare change – money that she had been able to "put aside."

Maybe the Market four blocks away had a big sale on apples, three cents cheaper than the store across the street. And the apples were just as good. And then there was the bruised fruit that was on "special." And what difference did it make if the fruit had a little spot or mark? When you ate it it was just as good.

So the pennies and even the nickels went into the sugar bowl, and as Mama was quick to point out, "From pennies come nickels...from nickels, quarters (she skipped the dimes) and from quarters, dollars."

And by the end of the year there was a tidy little hoard that had been accumulated. So you may well ask, what would Mama do with her little nest egg? She certainly never thought of spending it on herself. "The coat still keeps me warm and another house-dress who needs?"

And we never wanted for food. There was always the traditional three meals and milk and fresh-baked cookies at 3 o'clock when we came home from school. Our clothes might not have been new, but they were always clean – washed each night and put out on the line in the morning so that the fresh air would sanitize everything.

And as far as entertainment was concerned, there was always the library and the radio, although the latter was supervised and we were warned, "Enough already! You'll get glued to the box. Better read a book." But we pleaded and usually got dispensation for one more program if we assured her that we had finished all our homework and studied our spelling words.

So what extravagance did Mama have in mind? Well each year at "Holiday Time" Mama took the *peckel* of bills and coins and went to the big department store where there was a special sale and she would return with a scarf (part cashmere) or gloves. And then she went to the neighborhood bank, with the nice lady teller who lived in the yellow apartment house with the canopy, and got fresh dollar bills. This she placed in an envelope with a five cent greeting card that she bought in the candy store around the corner. All was wrapped in fancy paper and handed to Papa.

No, Dear Reader, you're wrong. It was not a gift for him. He was instructed (and there was no use arguing) to give the gift to the Union Delegate.

All comments ceased as Mama explained, "Gifts I don't need. I've got a good husband, nice children, a place to put my head at night. And without a paycheck each week, don't think about it. And then in Yiddish (worthy of the Yiddish Theater) she added, "*Az mir schmeart, fohrt mir.* All wheels need the grease."

So William Shakespeare could warn us that from nothing comes nothing, but Mama had already learned the lesson. Only she added, "The pennies in the bowl I don't need. Let Mrs. Rockefeller worry about where to buy a fur coat. Me, I'm a rich lady."

And you know, I never disagreed with my Mama, especially when she was hugging me.

The Importance of Breakfast

"Cholesterol? Not in our vocabulary..."

I think it was like the eleventh commandment. Every morning, after I took care of all my early morning responsibilities in our house, there was always a line-up to get into the bathroom. And because of my rank – I being the youngest – I always found myself at the end of the line.

No matter all my entreaties that this was an emergency... believe me... *zoll gornisht helfen*... all to no avail. I could yell and scream and dance and jump up and down and... you fill in the rest...all to no avail... I waited.

I sat down finally at the kitchen table and heard Mama inform everyone of the importance of eating a good breakfast. "Breakfast," she told everyone who would listen (and that meant everyone), "is the most important meal of the day. So eat...Eat."

Now, of course, throughout the day the message, though slightly altered, was repeated. Lunch became essential to give us strength, and three o'clock milk and cookies gave us the needed energy to play ball. And dinner – (or did we call it "supper?") – well, that was so vital because, how else would we grow big and strong?

And each food presented to us had some special value and importance. Milk was for strong bones and teeth; fish was brain food to keep us smart and so that

72

we could get 100's on the Friday white-paper tests; carrots gave us good eyes (did you ever see a rabbit with glasses? Ha... so!); and prunes were so that...well you all know what prunes were good for – they were to keep your system in good working order.

And with prunes there came a special ritual as well.

Now when we were children, milk came in bottles. And the first thing that Mama did was to open the bottle and skim the cream off the top. This cream was placed in a special pitcher and we knew that, first off, some went into Papa's coffee mug and then what was left over went on top of the stewed prunes.

Mama stewed the prunes several times a week and added raisins (also good for the body machinery because it contained iron) to this concoction. Then as this mixture was ladled out to us and we were urged to eat, some of this special creamy milk was used to top it all off.

Cholesterol? Not in our vocabulary. After all, we grew up on eggs, sour cream on the baked potato, sour cream with cottage cheese, sour cream with borsht, sour cream with sour cream. And to help clog up the arteries a bit more, there was butter, and chicken fat, and *grivenes* – that fried melange of chicken fat and onions.

But breakfast was special. We had to "fix ourselves" so that we could do well in school. Somehow the oatmeal, also laced with that special cream, and the bread and butter were essential elements for helping us to compete with the other kids whose Mamas were not so caring. (Were there any such?)

And bread, too, came with warnings. White bread was an absolute no-no. And to prove the point Mama would take a slice of white bread, if ever such an item slipped into our kitchen, and remove quite forcibly the inside soft piece section (that I loved) from the center and roll it up into a soft mush. And then Mama would pronounce, "See this is what you want to put into your stomach! *Pheh!*"

Then we would each be given a slice of whole wheat bread, *shmeared* with butter and some home-made jelly. And to wash it all down there was a glass of milk. I suppose that this was low-fat or no-fat milk (in later years Mama would call it "skinny" milk) since all the cream had been skimmed off.

And we knew full well that not a drop would remain in the glass, or a morsel of cereal in the bowl, or a crumb on the plate, or else there would be some unfortunate child in China who would die of malnutrition because of our utter disregard for food.

And after breakfast and the admonition to eat slowly, to chew our food carefully, to brush our teeth, not to rush – the teacher would wait for us – but still, Heaven forbid we should be late (match those two bits of advice, I dare you), to brush our shoes and comb our hair, not forget our homework – we were ready to leave and start the day.

Oh, but first, "Not such a hurry that you don't kiss your Mama and Papa goodbye."

Now that's better. So maybe this isn't a bad bit of advice to give to all parents today. A few prunes, a glass of milk and a kiss.

Let the day begin.

A Grandchild's Audition for "Stardom"

"It might not be my acting ability that caught her attention."

The smell of grease paint. The sound of applause. The curtain comes down, and then goes back up as the actors and actresses appear and take their final bows. Such excitement! A regular hooha!

And I suppose that this is the dream of every nine year old girl. At least it was the "cat-nap" if not the full fledged dream of Laurel, affectionately known by those within the circle as Libbe-Leah.

And so it came as no surprise that when the auditions took place on that eventful Sunday afternoon she appeared, flanked by siblings, parents, grandparents and even a few of the neighborhood friends – all coming to give her moral support – as she belted out with a voice that would raise the near-dead, "Tomorrow! Tomorrow!"

And if you think that this was a great moment for Bubbie and Zaydie, well you're not far off the mark. But still bear in mind that there were seventy other assorted young ladies ages six through goodness knows what who also ascended the pulpit – only now it was a stage – and they too were belting out the wonders and expectation of "Tomorrow" in hopes that they would succeed in being the perfect Annie. Such excitement!

I did my best to stay awake while the "others" auditioned and waited for my *ayn und ayntsigeh* (try that out for size) to be called upon. But the eyes were growing heavy despite the admonition of my own Annie not to embarrass the family by dozing off. And then the nine year old munchkin nuzzled up to me and asked if I would audition for a part.

"For Annie?" I asked with a little bit of surprise, "I don't think I have the qualifications."

"Oh Grandpa," she giggled, "not for Annie, for Daddy Warbucks. You'd be great."

For a minute I wallowed in her enthusiasm until I caught a glimmer of understanding as she eyed my follicly impoverished scalp and realized that it might not be my acting ability that had caught her attention.

And then finally after what seemed like a year and a *mit-vokch*, she (and you know who that pronoun refers to) was called. Slowly she ascended, with such grace and dignity. Of course, she had been primed for days by friends of the family, and now as she took measured steps, she was Queen Esther appearing before Ahasuerus to plead for her people (And if I perish, I perish). She was Deborah leading the frightened Israelites to victory. She was Miriam exulting with her maidens on dry land to the sound of drum and timbrel (Exactly what's a timbrel? No matter.) She was... no need to go on.

And then she looked at the audience of other aspiring actors and actresses flanked by parents, friends and a couple of extra bubbies and zaydies, and she established eye contact with (was it me? was it really me?) just as she had been advised by the "other Bubbie," and she sang and made a "joyful noise unto the Lord,"

"Tomorrow, Tomorrow, the sun will come out tomorrow..."

All right I know I'm becoming a bit theatrical, but

it's in the blood. She concluded the song without stumbling and if I could, I should have rushed up to the *bimah* with a dozen red roses. But I held myself back. After all there were other aspiring actresses, other hopefuls, to consider. And perish forbid I should injure the feeling of a budding thespian. Even if...

So now you want to know the conclusion. Enough with the overture and the introduction. The good news and the bad news. Well, the light of my life, my own Libbe-Leah, my Sarah Heartburn, did not get the lead. She was not chosen for the Little Orphan Annie, but she was picked to be part of the chorus.

And when I spoke to her – wondering how she would accept this "let-down," this mild rejection, I pointed out the value of being a part of the support group – that the whole was equal to the sum of its parts (how geometric of me, although I think that my point was lost) and how much I hoped that she would take this new responsibility as a challenge – I didn't get any tears or even a "whine'" or two of "It's not fair." She listened obediently and then said, "Isn't it great that I'm going to be part of the show!

"And you know what, Grandpa? I decided that when I grow up I'm going to be a teacher."

Good choice...

Mama Never Got A Diploma

"But there was a salary."

Mama never got a diploma. Not even from her elementary school. Secondary school was out of the question, because in those days – and now we're talking about the beginning of the twentieth century – when you had a teen-aged brother and a widowed mother (and you were a girl), well... Or as Mama would say in later years, "You became a drop-out – and that was before we even knew what "drop-out" meant. (And here I always thought that a Jewish drop-out was someone who stopped before he got his Ph.D.)

But to continue. Mama was just fourteen, actually fourteen and a month – but who's going to be a stickler when it comes to a lady's age – and she was in the eighth grade at P.S.2 on the Lower East Side of New York. (Schools didn't have names at that time, only numbers.)

Well, graduation exercises were just a week away and summer was approaching. (Such a hot June, it was, and who even heard of air conditioners?) And then one hot afternoon Mama was told that there was a store in the neighborhood, twelve blocks away – practically right around the corner – and they needed someone to work there – take care of cash, do stock, sweep floors, clean the windows, twelve hours a day, but you got Saturday (after all, that was Shabbos) off and on Sunday, only half a day to clean and take care that all the merchandise was in order for Monday.

But it was a job and that meant that Mama would be able to bring in money to support the family and that her brother would be able to continue with his studies and that there would be rent money and food money and maybe even a little left over at the end of the month to buy a new blouse when it was on sale.

But there was a hitch in all this excitement. Every silver lining, it appears, has a cloud. It was Friday when Mama was offered the job and she had to start working on the following Monday... at once. And "at once" meant 8:00 a.m. sharp – SHARP! Not a minute later.

And graduation was also on Monday...at 10:00 a.m. sharp. There was no compromise. No discussion. No bargaining. If you want the job, you get here ready to work on Monday. At 8:00 a.m. – sharp. You got it? End of story.

And so Mama went to work. She never told her family about the conditions or the graduation exercises. And there were no graduation exercises and no diploma – at least none for her. But there was a salary.

And her brother was able to continue his schooling – and even pick up a couple of his own diplomas on the road – and from high school, too! The last words were echoed by Mama many years later. And there was such pride and such joy and such love as she said those words.

But for Mama there was no diploma. And when I asked her many, many years later, years after the fact, if she had any regrets at all, she had no hesitation whatsoever in her voice. "Of course not. Why should I?"

So as I write this story and tell you about the diploma that was never given and that was never received, a diploma that was not awarded to a young girl who would have been so proud to hang it on the wall next to all the ones that years later were received by her children and her grandchildren, I too have no sadness. No sadness and no regrets. All right...so maybe a few.

3. Growing Up Jewish

Uncle Max — Who Is A Jew?

"The message didn't come from Mt. Sinai, but from Memphis."

My Uncle Max lived for most of his adult life in Memphis. So maybe you've heard of Memphis? No? Sure you did. That's where Elvis, the one who wiggled and jumped, made his home. So now you remember?

Well, to continue, Max (or as he was always called by Mama, his older sister, Maxie or *Maxele*) made his home in that southern community and came north to visit on a periodic (that usually meant twice a year) basis. We kids were always a little bit in awe of him. After all, he lived far away and yet seemed equally at home in the Bronx or in Manhattan – and no doubt, in Memphis as well.

He used to laugh whenever he walked with us on the Grand Concourse. "Here in the Bronx," he said, "you have more synagogues on one street than we have in the entire city where I live." (Oh how times have changed! The synagogues have been replaced with Video stores, Pizza Parlors, Chinese Restaurants and an occasional Baptist Church. But those were different days. Believe me. I'm telling you.)

When we asked the Good Uncle about the synagogues in Memphis, he told us that they had three synagogues, a Reform, a Conservative and an Orthodox.

I remember that we pre-adolescents, the know-it-alls of the neighborhood used to refer to the Reform Temple as the "Protestant *shul*." We used to peek through the windows because it had been rumored that the men didn't even wear yarmulkes! (Hard to believe.)

"Which one do you belong to?" I asked rather timidly because I wasn't sure if I should discuss religion. But Uncle Max had no problem in telling me, "Why, all three. They all need my support and help."

I later learned that he went to the Reform temple on Friday nights. (They had the best *onegs* following services.) He worshiped in the Conservative on the High Holy Days because that's where his best friend went. And when he had *yarhzeit* he attended the Orthodox synagogue.

The Orthodox synagogue was more than a *shul* – it was an imposing structure. What a building! And it had a name to match: the Baron DeHirsch Synagogue. (Wow! All the synagogues I knew had names like Young Israel or Zion Temple or Mt. Eden Center. But here was a name that made you think of royalty – a Baron! Wow! Double Wow! I was really impressed.) And then I timidly asked, "But which is the *real* synagogue? The *best* one, I mean."

It was then that I was given a lesson that has stayed with me. I learned that we needn't worry about which path is the real one, which road leads straight to Sinai. I was told that it was time that we Jews should stop worrying about which synagogue is the most holy, which prayer book contains the best prayers. Instead of worrying about what separates us and what divides us, better we should be concerned about what unites us and brings us together.

The message didn't come from Mt. Sinai, but from Memphis and I think that I gained extra respect for the carrier of the message that day, especially when he told me – even though I don't think I understood the full impact of his words until many years later – "Believe me *boichik*, if you are worried about who is a "real" Jew, don't let it bother you. There will be plenty of people – and I don't mean Jews – who will be quick to point out who is Jewish and who is not."

It was several months later in Europe that Jews around the world learned this lesson that I was taught by an uncle from Memphis, Tennessee.

"Shmearers" vs. Painters

"Today you don't find real workers any more."

"I would much rather move than paint," said Mama as she uttered a sigh that conveyed that all the problems of the world were upon her shoulders. Papa just made little guttural noises and retreated to the newspaper. Every year it was the same.

Once a year, the painters came and did the kitchen and bathroom, and every three years, it was a general over-all painting of the entire apartment. And Mama always complained.

When Papa was not around (lucky for him) she met with Tanta Pesha. "*Oy*, Pesha, they're coming next Tuesday." The "they" referred to the painters. "I said that I wanted only one man. This way I can keep an eye on what he's doing."

Pesha nodded. "A lot of good it will do you. The paint they use. *Pheh* – like water. They call it white but it turns yellow before it touches the walls. And if you ask for two coats, you'd think that you were asking for gold."

Mama and Pesha sighed in unison. "Painters? – No. *Shmearers* – that's what they are."

And yet when the painters arrived, both of them, two men, Mama was all sweetness and light. "Oh, I see you brought a helper, how nice. Maybe I can make you a sandwich. Fresh brisket on rye bread. I'll put a little lettuce on it. It's good for you. You've got to keep up your strength. Painting is a hard job believe you me."

And while the workers ate, Mama made her requests. "The window sills need scraping and could you cover the cracks in the ceiling?" And the painters painted (or as Mama told Tanta Pesha, "*shmeared*") and Mama watched, pointing out where they missed a spot or where the paint didn't quite cover.

But sometimes – most of the time, Mama got her way.

And then there was Cousin Hymie. Hymie was a painter too, only Mama called him a "real painter, not a *shmearer*." But he lived in Brooklyn and to travel all the way to the Bronx, well that was too much to ask. But still when Cousin Hymie appeared, he came paint brush in hand.

And while Mama and Anna shared a *glezzele* tea and some honey cake – so fresh that it practically melts before you taste it – Hymie repainted the kitchen set. Each year it was a different color, one year red, one year white, one year yellow.

Hymie was an artist, a real painter, and he took pride in his work. And Mama always made certain to admire his craft.

"Today you don't find real workers any more. Nobody takes care," she lamented. "See," she pointed out to me, "real paint and it doesn't drip on the linoleum."

And my brother and I agreed, although I somehow wished that we could have kept the yellow, but Mama said the white goes with everything and would brighten up the kitchen.

The years have passed and Cousin Hymie and his beautiful Anna are no longer around. Not even in Brooklyn. Their little boy, Jerry is now called Chuck (explain that one) and lives somewhere on the Island. He's probably my age or maybe a bit younger and I wonder if he remembers that his father was a real painter, an artist, and not a *shmearer*, that he took pride in his work.

And that's what I hope to impart to the young people who come to my class, that when they enter their professions, they too must have pride so that the paint doesn't drip and the cracks get covered, that the window sills need scraping. And this applies to the doctors and the lawyers (I hope my kids are listening), to the computer experts and the plumbers (we called them *plum-bers*), to the salespeople and the writers. Yes and to the teachers and professors, too.

After all, we need them all. So let them take pride. *Shmearers* we have enough already.

A Bris & A Nosh

"The first time they have wine,
they associate it with … you know."

Tanta Pesha came scurrying (that's even faster than hurrying) down the street to the apartment house in which she lived.

But before she could enter, Lilly With The Hair intercepted her. Lilly was sitting on an egg crate in front of the building, a shopping cart flanking her left side. "So what's the big rush?" she asked. "Tell me, you're going or you're coming? And why are you so dressed up? A hat and a blue suit. So *ois-ge-pitzt*. Maybe it's a *Yom-Tov* that I missed? At four in the afternoon, who wears a hat going to the supermarket? Even when there's a special on cottage cheese."

Tanta Pesha slowed down to a complete stop. "So since you ask me I'll tell you. Not from the supermarket, but practically a *Yom-Tov*." She paused. It was one of those enigmatic pauses that she was so good at. Then she continued, "Actually I'm coming from a *bris*. My nephew Velvel."

Lilly looked astonished, "Velvel? Chanah Rivka's son? That nice boy who got married to the Jewish girl from the old country? A nice boy with a good job – the one they call Warren – and I heard he bought a house somewhere. But a *bris*!"

Pesha saw the look in Lilly's eyes and was quick to explain, "Not his, of course not at his age *vay iz mir*. He has a son, a sweet little *boychikel*. And they're calling him Maxie, after the uncle from Memphis. For a minute I thought they were going to name him Elvis when they were talking about Memphis."

She gave a chuckle, pleased at her own humor. "But Max I like. Better than what Fat Rosie's nephew did, naming a child Simpson so you can't tell if it's a boy or a girl, and then the *Mohel* had to tell us that it was a boy after he looked. But this was such a nice affair. You want to hear?"

Lillie gave her a look that indicated, "Why not?" And so Pesha told of the *Mohel* who came with a long gray beard that went down to his *pupik* and who looked like he was as old as Macushleh but who was only a little past forty and he had already seven children and the oldest wasn't even a bar mitzvah yet and the youngest was just a year and his wife was expecting this October. (And here she took a breath.)

And then she continued, "And he asked for a *tallis* and when I said 'Was this part of the tradition?,' he said, 'No, but it looks good on the pictures when you take them.' And you know he was right!"

Then Pesha went on, "Such a sense of humor he had. When one of the friends who works with the father asked the *Mohel* if circumcision was painful, he was told that after this *bris*, he didn't expect the baby to walk for at least nine months!"

And Lillie With The Hair began to laugh and then she became serious. "But tell me, everything came off all right? *Oy vey*! You should pardon the expression. I meant if everything was good – with the baby I mean."

Pesha reassured her that the baby was fine, "A little wine on the lips and he stopped crying. No wonder Jews don't become *shikkurs*, the first time they have wine they associate it with...you know." And indeed Lillie did know.

And then Pesha concluded, "And the food was

delicious. The apple cake I made melted in your mouth and the "appetizing" was so fresh, it was all finished except for the carrot salad – which in my opinion had too much mayonnaise, just if you happen to ask. And better they could have made some herring salad like my Tanta Shosha, may she rest in peace, used to make with beets and apples. But no one asked my opinion. So as you know, I don't, but when I'm not asked. Not that there wasn't enough to eat, but still a little herring salad on a piece of fresh rye bread would have hit the spot."

Lillie understood and so offered a bit of sage advice. "So you know what? We should live and be well. At the bar mitzvah, you'll make the herring and I'll bring the rye bread."

And Tanta Pesha with a sigh of contentment quickly said, "Now, Lillie, you speak like a smart woman. But we don't have to wait for the bar mitzvah because in my ice box there's some chopped herring made exactly like my Tanta Shosha, may she rest in peace, used to make. And if I'm not mistaken there's also some rye bread, even the *krychick*, in the bread box. So come and join me – unless you have a hot date."

"At my age, herring is better than a hot date that I don't have even." And the two went together with the shopping cart trailing behind.

What's In A Name?

"He was dubbed "The Loksh" because of his resemblance to a long noodle."

Tanta Pesha couldn't wait to call me. Such excitement! Her cousin, "the one who moved from Queens, you remember her – she had two daughters – one who was not so *Ay-yi-yi* and the other a real beauty. Well the rather plain one (see, I'm being diplomatic) was married recently and she had just given birth."

I expressed my delight. After all, a new child in the family is always a wonderful event. And then I added, "That's great. I just remembered she just got married."

Tanta Pesha added with a knowing wink in her voice (explain that image, if you can), "Well this is a *zibitel*. And if you want me to be exact, a six-month baby. But all is well, and I'm sure that all the others will take a full nine months."

I didn't ask for a course in biology, sociology, or mathematics. It was easier simply to say, "So what's the name. Do I buy blue or pink?"

Tanta Pesha was fast. "Blue. A little boy, with a lot of hair. No wonder she had such heartburn all through the pregnancy. And we'll have to wait for the *bris* to find out the name."

I hoped that it would be a nice name. I sort of remembered all the names in the family. And all the people that we knew. Oh my. I winced. We all

remember Fat Rosie In Apartment 3-C, the one who
talks on the phone all day. And then there was The
Greener. She was a cousin whose name I will never
know but she was always called The Greener because
she spoke with a heavy inflection, a carry-over from the
time when she came to America from "the Old
Country."

And of course there was Alta Maxie, who was
distinguished from Maxie The Funferrer. The latter had
a stutter that always got in his way whenever he told
one of his interminably long stories. Actually I later
learned that the Alta Maxie was three years younger
than the Funferrer, but why be exact?

And so to continue, in the family there was a nice
gentleman who married three times, but not all at once,
and was always called The Uncle. When I asked Pesha
what his name was she said, "Who?" and I said, "The
Uncle." And she said, "That's it – the Uncle. Why do
you ask? You already know." I didn't pursue that one.

And let me not overlook poor Sarah who was called
by all Sarah The Meese, because she was rather
homely. (Again I'm being kind.)

And we always shortened her name so that we
always heard, "Tell me did you speak to The Meese
recently? How is she doing?"

I was warned not to shorten her name in her
presence. But that was better than the cousin known as
Rivke The *Trayfe*. I always surmised that she received
this appellation because she was rather lax in her
observance of dietary laws. But Pesha informed me that
it was only the family's way of distinguishing her from
Frume Rivke who actually was less scrupulous but...
another story that Pesha never concluded.

And then there was always Uncle Izzy, tall and
gaunt, who was always referred to as The Loksh – or
even The Langer Loksh. It took me years to find out
that his real name was Irving (really it's Isadore, but he

wants to sound like a Yankee!) and so when he was dubbed The Loksh because of his resemblance to a long noodle, there was some kind of nominal retribution.

So we are told by our sages that a good name is more precious than fine oil. And those wise men had a point there. So what if Moses becomes Mervyn or Feigel becomes Filomena or Benjamin becomes Barton? It's the thought that counts, isn't it?

So now you want me to tell you the conclusion of the story. Well, the little boy, the *zibitel*, he who was born rather quickly after the marriage benedictions were recited, was named Jacob – after his uncle Clifford.

Doggie Bags, Mitzvahs, & Free Samples

'But if it's all the same to you, we prefer to pick our own."

Lillie With The Nails was almost out of breath as she hurried over to the park bench where the "Ladies" were sitting. "Such a day," said Tillie, "like a gift. Take advantage. *Nu*, Lillie? Take a load off and sit down. There's no charge. Here sit by Rosie. There's plenty of room."

Lillie followed direction and heaved a sigh that came from the depths of her being. *"Oy vay,"* she uttered, and immediately Gertie with the Hair took the cue, "So what's the matter, Lillie... a problem with the children? Someone sick, God forbid?"

"Nothing's wrong, thanks God, but you wouldn't believe. Last night my daughter Sarah With The "H" decided to take me out to dinner, even though I told her that what do we have to go out for and spend money when I could just as easy make something?" Open a can of salmon or scramble some eggs.

"But she insisted, so we went to the new place that opened up where the Kosher Deli used to be and is now out of business. They couldn't make out ever since his wife got so sick and the daughter got in a family way."

Everyone looked concerned. "The daughter, she's married?" asked Fat Rosie From Apartment 3-C. Lillie

93

gave a look of scorn. "Married? Not even engaged. But she lives with that skinny boy from New Jersey. Children today! I can't understand them at all."

"So you went to the New Place to eat?" asked Gertie, "It was good?"

Lillie immediately came back on track, "Good? *Pheh...* terrible. The food was like poison – such small portions! But the place was so crowded, like they were giving it away. All the early birds were there. And when it came time to leave, I didn't even think there would be enough in my doggie bag to feed a canary. But why should I leave food to go to waste? So I took home the rolls and half a baked potato."

The ladies were interested. "The rolls were good?" Lillie acknowledged, "Not bad. At least they were fresh and the onion rolls, except for too much salt that I have to watch because of my pressure, well I took home the two that were left."

Everyone seemed to understand. "And you know who I saw there?" She didn't wait for a reply. "The Brown Sisters."

Gertie was quick to interject. "I see them every Friday at *shul*. They're the first to get to the *oneg* after services. Even before the Rabbi gives the blessing, already they're on their feet."

Rosie took a deep breath, "So maybe you heard what happened to me, what I did, two weeks ago?"

It was time for true confessions and everyone was listening, so now that she was assured of an audience, she continued.

"You know how the Brown Sisters are always taking home a napkin with cookies 'for later.' Well sometimes I even see them with a little plastic baggy so that if there's fruit salad, they can load up and they always explain that it tastes better the next day. Well last week, there was this big service and I was helping out with the Sisterhood to set up the tables for the *oneg*, and I knew that there would be a big crowd so I thought to myself, 'Rosie, do a *mitzvah*, and I made a little bag of cookies, the ones with the cherries and the chocolate filling, and I added a few of the brownies and even a piece of the special coffee cake, and when the Brown Sisters came in, I told them that I had a doggie bag for them."

Everyone looked at Rosie with a tinge of admiration, but she dispelled the look when she added, "and you think that they were pleased? Not on your life! The older one, the one with the eyes, looked at me and said, "Thank you very much, but if it's all the same to you, we prefer to pick our own." And there I was left holding the bag."

All the Ladies looked at each other not knowing how to respond until Tanta Pesha, who until now was sitting quietly and taking in the afternoon sun, smiled her special smile, and said, "So you know what they say – 'No good deed goes unpunished.' And that goes for *mitzvahs* as well. But I'm sure that the bag of cookies didn't go to waste."

There was silence and then she added, "and she married the skinny boy from New Jersey and they're opening up a new deli near the park. And what's more they're giving out free samples next week."

Pesha was a regular font of knowledge. And when she added, "So maybe we'll all go to wish them well..." who could disagree?

The Bar Mitzvah Speech Bribe

"And after services, I'll bring my chopped liver, made from my mother's secret recipe..."

I remember... Oh how I remember... I was approaching my thirteenth birthday and was about to celebrate that "day of days" – marking the beginning of manhood for a Jewish boy. (Now you know I am not discussing puberty, but if you ask, I might just do that in another story.)

I was getting ready for my Bar Mitzvah at Zion Temple on the Grand Concourse and Tremont Avenue (of course in the Bronx, but I didn't have to tell you that) and I had my "interview" with the kindly Rabbi Green. And when I came home I announced in a squeaky pre-adolescent falsetto, "No Bar Mitzvah!"

And when Mama blanched, I repeated, only this time an octave lower and a decibel higher, "No, no, no! No Bar Mitzvah!"

Mama sat down. I remained standing, and then came the explanation. I had gone to the Rabbi's office for a "run-through" since my ceremony was only three weeks away. I chanted all the requisite portions and displayed my proficiency in reading from the Torah and Rabbi Green kept saying "Fine, fine, fine." And once in a while he added, "Good."

And as I relayed this information, Mama said, "So everything was fine and good. So what's with the big No-no-no?"

And then I dropped the shoe. It was "the speech." I wanted to write my *own* speech and the Rabbi insisted that I read a *prepared* speech. And this I would not accept.

And so Mama put on her good dress and her *Shabbos* hat and went with me to the Big Synagogue and straight into the Rabbi's office.

He explained that maybe I could write a speech – after all, I was a good student in the Hebrew school – but what about all the others? Soon everyone would want to write a speech and what would that lead to?

He was adamant and so was I. And as Mama left the office she said, "We'll discuss this with Poppa." I was sure that I was in for it and that there would be arm-twisting and promises and bribes and tears.

But no. To my surprise both Mama and Poppa agreed with me. Mama said, "A Bar Mitzvah only comes once and the child should have his day." And I was the child and this was my day.

And so came the solution. The next day, flanked by Mama and Poppa, we went to the little shul on Eastburn Avenue. Actually it was a two room affair. You walked down two steps into a small apartment someplace between the ground floor and the basement. It was half submerged and there was a room where a very limited group of men (and perhaps a few wives) met to hold services.

We knew this synagogue since very often when they couldn't gather together ten men for a minyan, the Rabbi's grandson, a boy a year older than I, would be sent out to recruit willing (or not so willing) males over the age of thirteen, calling out, "We need you. It's a mitzvah." (Some of the older kids used to hide when they saw him coming.)

And to this boy's grandpa, a venerable Rabbi who was full-bearded and whose glasses rested on his nose, we explained the problem. The old man listened, shaking his head and making no comment. And then Poppa (I never appreciated how wise he was) stated the clincher – "And I'll do my best to come to morning minyan for at least a month and, who knows, maybe more. And I'll make a nice contribution." And Mama added, "And after services I'll bring my chopped herring, made from my mother's secret recipe, and my gefilte fish and sponge cake and honey cake… the kind with raisins…"

And Poppa added, "And four bottles of sweet wine."

Perhaps it was the wine or maybe the honey cake with raisins or the secret recipe for chopped herring (although it would be nice to believe that the Rabbi recognized the need to bring another young Jew into the Covenant), but whatever it was, the old man rubbed his beard, wiped his glasses, and looked at me straight into my moist eyes and said in a voice that was something like the way the Prophets of old must have sounded, "So why not! *Far vuss nit?*"

And so that November I became Bar Mitzvah – in a little shul on Eastbum Avenue – and not in the very big synagogue on the Grand Concourse with the beautiful wooden pews and the stained glass windows. Instead, I delivered my speech to friends and invited guests who sat on folding chairs in a room that was something between a cellar and a musty hall, and I chanted from a beautiful Torah scroll and recited a speech that I had written.

And all the people, even the Rabbi and his grandson, said I was terrific. Only maybe they said it in Yiddish. And then the Rabbi embraced me and said I was a man. But first he told Mama that the chopped herring was the best he ever tasted and the Rebbitzen wanted the recipe.

And I never found out if Mama gave it to her. After all, there are limits.

Keeping Kosher At Someone Else's Home

"Sometimes it's more important what comes out of your mouth than what goes in."

The year I entered junior high school, I learned several important lessons that have remained with me throughout my life.

The first I discovered on my own – girls are not simply soft boys. (I shall not pursue this bit of sage understanding at this moment, but shall wait until the children leave the room. Otherwise I shall have to resort to speaking Yiddish.)

And the second involves my dilemma concerning Jewish ritual. On this latter aspect, I admit freely it was my mother who taught me to adhere to two basic tenets of what she called *menshlichhkeit*. And of this I shall write.

It was during these formative years that I became confused about necessary rituals I had to adhere to in order to be what my Hebrew school teacher called "a good Jew." And indeed I began to wonder about what – or who – was a Jew.

In Hebrew school, this was a big concern. We spoke of the importance of the mother's religion and the mystique that only if your mother was Jewish, could you be Jewish. Little did we know that one day this big dispute about what qualifies a person to be a Jew would spring forth to trouble the Jewish community. (Nor did we foresee that, at that very moment in Nazi Germany, there were those deciding that even if one of your grandparents were Jewish... and you know that story, unfortunately.) But then this was one of the questions that "troubled" some of the guys who wore *yarmulkes* and went to the *yeshiva* and played on my stickball team.

And so every once in a while when there was a lull in the conversation (like we didn't have enough to worry about) and we couldn't decide who was the best pitcher on the Yankees, someone would point out that there was a rumor that one of the boys on our team wasn't really Jewish, since they had heard that his great-grandmother on his mother's side, a woman who had long since left this vale of tears (how's that for an image for twelve-year- olds to contend with?), had not been a member of the faith.

And so I decided to take this problem to Mama, since I had a feeling that discussing the theological implications with the Rabbi or Hebrew school teacher would cause me no end of grief and make me miss the choosing-up of teams.

It was at that moment that I was taught one of the two precepts that has stuck with me – "If someone says he's Jewish, don't ask questions. That person is Jewish. Forget about the grandmas and grandpas. He *is* what he *does*."

It was years later that I read about Ruth in the Bible and learned that if you called yourself Jewish and cast your lot (this was the lesson for *Shavuos*, not *Purim*) with the Jewish people, then even you could become the Bubbie or Grand-bubbie of someone like King David. Not a bad lesson. ("She was what she did.")

And the second lesson? That occurred when I became concerned about keeping kosher and what to eat when I was invited to someone's home.

Mama kept a scrupulously kosher cuisine and so I became concerned about what would happen to my eternal soul if I ate a forbidden food, even by error, at some friend's home. The Rabbi told me that the answer to my dilemma was simple. "When in doubt, don't eat."

But for a growing adolescent, this was a tough dictum to swallow. (Another interesting image.) So once again I went to Mama. She did not hesitate to give a response. "Don't look in someone else's pot," she said, letting me know that it was enough if someone gave me food that they said was ritually correct, and that I didn't need to question the authenticity of the pots and pans. And then she added for good measure, "Sometimes it's more important what comes out of your mouth than what goes in." Again some sage advice from a lady who never attended secondary school.

Now I know there will be many who will look askance at Mama's religious philosophy and wonder how these two pieces of "wisdom" could match up with a person who lived all her life within the confines of tradition. And yet, if you will allow me, as I have grown older, I wonder if there is not much to be gained by not looking into corners to disenfranchise and to separate, to alienate and to shun. And when I doubt – perhaps it might be just as well not to look into everyone's pots – but to be more concerned with what is cooking on one's own stove.

These were the lessons that have stayed with me from my early teens. These – and the knowledge of what is the big difference between boys and girls.

Which is more important? Well, you decide.

And "The Kid" Makes A Minyan

"Kid! That's what he called me!"

The phone rang. And even before I could pick up the receiver (before the third ring, no less) the voice in the other room called out, "Who could be calling now?"

The last word had a definite emphasis as if indicating that four-thirty in the afternoon was such an unusual hour for any human being to try to establish contact with another human being. A number of answers raced through my mind if I wanted to respond to the question. Which I didn't.

It could be our daughter wanting to know if I could run down to the grocery to pick up a container of milk. The regular kind. Because they're all out and she's in the middle of making dinner and the four-year-old fell asleep on the floor in the family room.

Or it could be that lady from that telephone company trying to persuade me to change my long distance carrier because now they're preparing to offer me two hundred free hours of calls (provided I call between 2:00 a.m. and 4:00 a.m. on any week without a national holiday and I don't speak for more than four minutes) and this is a special never-to-be-repeated offer that is only given once, but if I say 'no' they'll call back next week when we're in the middle of dinner.

Or it could be the young man who is taking a survey and needs just three minutes of my time and he won't ask any personal questions, but the first two questions are "How old are you?" and "How much do you earn a week?" Not personal? *Pheh!*

Or it could be, "Could I speak to Phyllis?" And I stop saying that there's no Phyllis living here and instead say, "She has been arrested for child molestation and is awaiting arraignment at the local police station."

Enough already! It's the third ring and so I pick up and hear the voice (the unmistakable voice, I might add. And I do.) of Abe from the local synagogue. And I know he's going to ask me to be part of the evening *minyan*. I know this even before he has a chance to say, "Hello. How are you?"

So I say, "Fine, Abe. I'll be right over." And he says, "This is Abe." And I say, "I know. I'm on my way."

So he responds, "This is Abe from the *shul*." And so I play the game and say, "OH, hello Abe. How are you?" "Don't ask," he tells me. (And now I'm sorry I asked.)

And after he tells me, he says that they need an extra man for the evening minyan and could I see my way clear... etc., etc. And even when I tell him that I'm on my way, he continues to tell me how important it is to be part of the congregation, but by now I'm out the door.

The first man to greet me as I entered the *shul* was Abe himself, a gentle, kind and pious man whose face lit up when he saw me and I could see that his mind was making a quick count on how many people were now present. The halo above his cherubic face lit up as he announced, "The kid makes number 10."

Kid! My day was made. Whatever else would take place, this was no doubt the highlight and I would repeat the comment over and over to all those who cared (and even those who did not) to listen.

"Now we don't have to call the neighbor," exulted

David, who was second in command.

"The neighbor?" Everyone looked puzzled and Abe asked, "He's Jewish?"

David was positive, "Jewish? He's very Jewish."

Everyone appeared relieved. "So maybe next time." And so the service began and as I sat (or stood...whatever...) and listened to the familiar words – the refrains chanted by Rabbi and Hazzan and then repeated by the group (and, hey, that meant ME) – I was transported to other days when I really was the kid and sometimes was corralled to be part of a *minyan*... and then there were other faces and other people other voices and other smiles.

And as these memories cavorted in my brain, I realized that the faces may change but the words remained and it was the words that formed the melody that connected me. And I think that my own voice grew stronger throughout that brief service and I have to admit that I walked home, after the conclusion, with an extra bounce to my gait – a special melody rolling about my brain, and an Abie-smile on my face.

I couldn't wait to tell the family, "Kid! Kid! That's what he called me. Let me tell you..."

Abe you did a real mitzvah today. God bless you.

And I'm sure He did.

Tanta Pesha and Looking Good on Shabbos'

"Where should I be going?
To a dance hall you think?

As soon as I came in, I could see there was a problem. It didn't take too much insight to diagnose the look on Tanta Pesha's face. There was something that was bothering her and I knew that I could never rest easy until I found out (she certainly wouldn't let me) and help to alleviate the situation. So I girded my loins (I'm not sure how one does that, but in the Bible I have read how many of the heroes of old would gird their loins when entering into a hazardous fray) and asked, "So tell me, what is the problem?"

Tanta Pesha looked up, "Better not to ask. Nothing so important, believe me."

I waited. I knew she would continue. I was right. "I need an opinion…" she said, "…the blue with the collar, the red flowers, or the black with the buttons?"

Now I was genuinely confused. Blue, black, red. I decided to keep still and wait until some explanation would emerge from the maze of colors. But none was forthcoming so I prodded – just a bit, "Blue? Black? I'm confused. "

"Me too," said Pesha. "What should I wear? I want I should look nice."

Now I was a bit curious, so I asked, "Where are you

going? Someplace special? A wedding? A bar mitzvah?" Yet I knew that if it were to some special event, I should have been informed. There was no way out. I had to ask, "Tell me, what's the special event? Where are you going?"

Tanta Pesha gave a small smile, "On *Shabbos*, where should I be going? To a dance-hall, you think? Or maybe on a cruise ship? To *shul* of course."

I knew that there was more to the story, so all I had to add was one word, "And...?"

She nibbled at the bait. "They're having a special *kiddush* to honor that Henry. The one whose children live near you. You know the daughter, the one who works and keeps herself so nice. And such a *ballabusta* – from her floor you could eat – so clean she keeps her house. And always a smile."

As I tried to reconstruct the image of the attractive woman with the clean floors, Pesha continued. "So it's her father, *oy* such a handsome man, a widower, he lost his wife – a really fine lady *nisht by unz gedacht* – but he keeps busy, what with his golf and his walking. So fast he walks on the boardwalk even Skinny Louie, the one who's always in the gym on the machines – and he's not even ninety yet – he can't keep up with Henry."

I finally found out that it was Henry's birthday and all the ladies of the area had 'their cap set.' Or as Tanta Pesha informed me, "Lillie, With The Red Nails bought a new dress at the 'fat lady's store,' not that it will do her any good, and Gussie With The Hair is going to spend all day Friday in the new beauty parlor. But who cares? Still I don't want to look like a second-hand dish rag in the *shul*, so I'll wear my hat with the little bow – and which dress – maybe the blue with the collar. It makes me look tall. Yes?"

I didn't respond. There was really no reason to, because Pesha was quick to tell me, "You've been such a help. I needed a man's opinion. You know I don't want to look too *shlumpy*, like I'm going to the supermarket, but still I don't want to look like I'm off to the White House either. You understand."

I did and told her so, but then I added with a smile, "Still you want this Handsome Henry to notice you. Maybe even bring you a cup of Sanka at the *Kiddush*?"

First Tanta Pesha's eyes opened wide, as if to say "What are you talking about?" But then there came that small smile on her face and a little light in her eyes,

"Look, at my age," she philosophized, "I don't need a date, even with a fine man like this Henry, God bless him, but... "

And now came that special pause before the clincher, "Still... if he asked, why should I refuse?"

Why indeed?

Yiddish Theater and The "Truth"
"The rules of the theater were all forgotten."

T he theater! Such magic! Even today, whenever I have the good fortune to go to the theater, I am overwhelmed by the feeling that I am entering a world of imagination... a world that I have been given the rare delight of viewing because a multitude of people – writers, actors, stage people – have joined together for my pleasure. I know, too, that the theater is not real. It's a world that exists only in the imagination of the viewer.

And so a little lesson before we begin. (So you thought we had already begun! Not at all, this was only the prologue to the imperial act. Aha!)

When the audience views what is happening on the stage, they must suspend their disbelief. There are only three walls in the room. Now we all know that each room (at least the ones I have) have four walls, or else think of all those peeping Toms! *Vay iz mir*! But in the theater we are all Peeping Tommies or else how could we know what's going on, on the stage?

So that is lesson number one. We must accept the three-walled room when we watch a play.

Lesson two is that there must never be communication between the actors and the audience. Actors speak to actors and there is an invisible wall (so many walls!) between the actor on stage and the patron in the audience. You agree? Then you have never been to the Yiddish theater. Not so, here. And now comes the story.

When I was just a little boy, not even a bar mitzvah, Mama and Papa used to take me on special occasions like my birthday or Chanukah or Purim or the second Sunday after *Shabbos Shuvah* (so I exaggerate a little) to the Second Avenue Theater to see a Yiddish play. I think that this was the time before babysitters and what else do you do with an eight-year-old or even a nine-year-old who could get into mischief at the drop of a *dreidel*. You *schlep* him with you and say, "Come. You'll like it."

And I did. I fell in love with Mollie Picon when she cavorted on the stage telling the audience in song *Der gantze velt iz a tay-ater."* And indeed the *"whole world was a theater."*

And I loved Yiddle with the Fiddle. I wept when the heroine was deserted by the no-goodnik who took advantage of her. (Mama how did she get a baby? Is she married?)

And I was introduced to Shakespeare – Shakespeare in Yiddish. There was *der Tochter fun Shylock*. You can keep The Merchant of Venice. For sheer pathos you have to witness Shylock grieving over his daughter who ran off with that Italian. A *shandeh*!

And then there was *Der Koenig Lear*, my favorite because it starred the second (or maybe even the first but who's counting?) great love of my life, Celia Adler, as the beautiful Cordelia. Now here comes the clincher.

When King Lear, bereft of family and deserted by his two daughters – such *chaleryas* that caused him so much misery – lets out a sigh and exclaims, "How sharper than a serpent's tooth to have a thankless child!" (and all this in Yiddish!) – the rules of theatergoing were all forgotten...that distance between audience and actor disappeared...and everyone around me, weeping and sobbing (and such a blowing of noses!) called out, *"Dos iz der emes!" "It's the truth, the honest truth!"*

And as we left the theater (I think it was the Second Avenue Theater. Yes, Sibby?) we felt that we had not been viewers or even eavesdroppers on life. We were part of life. We had been miraculously drawn into the world of the *shtetl* or the life of a particular family with *tsorris* that we shouldn't know from, but that we did. And so it was not unusual for Mama to turn to Papa and ask, "So what do you think will happen next?

Will the father be reconciled with the daughter? Will the no-good boy friend return and assume responsibility? Will the landlord repent and show mercy?

And Papa, always the realist, would say, "It's a play; it's only a play."

And many years later when the nine-year-old had grown up and recognized that it was only a play – but he still went to the theater, and although he missed the good old days with Mollie Picon and Menashe Skulnik and the beautiful Celia Adler – he wondered if he could teach young people the thrill of Shakespeare and Marlowe, Arthur Miller and Tennessee Williams.

And then one beautiful day while lecturing in class about the tragedy of Lear and the disappointment in his daughters and the alienation of parent and children, there came a sigh from the back of the class as I read the phrase "To have a thankless child..." I could have sworn I heard, *Es Ia verdad. Der Emes. The truth.*

4. Old Times
in the Old Jewish
Neighborhood

Leaving the Old Neighborhood
"But that's life. Nothing stays the same."

Now tradition has it that we must make three "trips" to Jerusalem each year for the Festivals. So when Tanta Pesha told me that she had taken Mama on a "trip," I listened most attentively. Since there had been no talk of passports or visas or even which airline had the cheapest ... oops I should have written most "economical"... flight, several places were immediately ruled out.

But I was prepared for the next question. "So guess where we went?" I decided not to opt for Lebanon or Libya (at least not at this time of the year) and Algeria was a no-no, so I felt it was better to ask, "Where?"

Tanta Pesha was quick. "You'll never guess. Never in a hundred years." (Now, I thought maybe Algeria wasn't so far-fetched.) Instead all I said was, "So tell me." There was a victorious smile on Pesha's face as she informed me, "I took your Mama back to the Old Neighborhood."

Now I must take a minute to explain. The "old" neighborhood was separated from the "new" neighborhood, where they currently lived by no great body of water, no ocean, no river, no lake, no stream. There were no mountain ranges in between to serve as barriers. In fact you didn't need to take a train or even a bus. A short walk of perhaps five or six blocks would take you there, although as Tanta Pesha was quick to point out, "There are two big intersections where they drive like crazy and you have to look both ways before crossing."

Tanta Pesha started her talk. "You should see the changes! You wouldn't recognize the place. First of all The Bakery expanded. It took over the candy store and I hear they hired a baker who has a specialty for raisins. Everything is raisins now. Even the bagels. And the store with Lady's dresses... closed. What a shame. Now it's a dollar store, where everything is a dollar except what you want and that's whatever price they want to charge. Believe me, I liked better the Lady's store. And the Little Shul ... no more. Terrible. And the poor Rabbi, such a nice fellow ... *oy!*"

I winced. I remembered the Rabbi most fondly. He was a man in his seventies and I saw the tears welling in Pesha's eyes, so I asked, "Was it sudden?"

Tanta Pesha dried her eyes with a tissue that she fished out of her pocket. "I'm all choked up," she said. "I spoke to his daughter-in-law and she told me that all of a sudden without warning, he packed up and moved to… to… Brooklyn."

I breathed a sigh of relief, but Pesha continued. "Brooklyn! Why Brooklyn? Who's there?" But she became philosophical. "But that's life. Nothing stays the same. And the Big Shul is fixing up the basement for catering. They took in new members, maybe from the Little Shul."

I moved to change the topic. Little, Big, it was getting to me, and somehow I was relieved to know that the kindly Rabbi had moved to Brooklyn and not... well... "Any other changes?" I asked.

Pesha was quick, "So many. Even your Mama's apartment. On the windows – blue curtains. Who heard of blue curtains? And upstairs the Lady with the Jewish name, the one who lost her husband, well not lost exactly, he ran off with the manicurist, but she preferred to say… you remember… so we all said she lost… anyway now she moved away to who knows where… maybe Yonkers – a regular wilderness – not near even a supermarket – and a lady schoolteacher moved in and she has plants on her window."

I was getting completely confused. My mind was still on the manicurist who ran off with the deceased husband with the blue curtains… no that was Mama's apartment… it was the one with a Jewish name."

Tanta Pesha rescued me. "Such a day we had. We even stopped in at the luncheonette – only now it's a donut store and we had a cup of coffee, but Mama had without the caffeine, she watches herself – and then this new owner gave us free samples of his donuts to wash down. And you know they were good – not greasy. We told him so and he told us he comes from some island, and Mama offered to bring back her *ruggelach* to him. Such a day.

"But you know, *Dahling* (again with the capital "D"), when we got back to your Mama's apartment, you know what she said? It's good to get away, but really there's no place like home…"

And both Tanta Pesha and I agreed that that was the truth.

The Candy Store —
From Treats to "Chatschkas"

"Every shelf was laden with treasures…"

"You wouldn't believe what I found in the Dollar Store," Fannie told her friends sitting in front of the yellow building with the awnings. "Look," she exclaimed as she pulled out a brown paper bag from her shopping cart.

"So what is it already?" Fat Rosie From Apartment 3-C wanted to know. And at this bit of needless coaxing, out came a little glass animal. Fannie held the figure carefully and showed it around, allowing each of the ladies to hold it, but each one being cautioned, "Be careful. You shouldn't drop. It's made from glass."

After a few semi-admiring looks, Tanta Pesha remarked, "So tell me, Fannie, another *chatschka* you need? What for? Already your apartment looks like a candy store on the Grand Concourse."

And now the memory and the explanation. The Grand Concourse you already know. It was the wide avenue that traversed the Bronx from North to South, modeled after the Champs-Elysee of Paris I'm told. (So hoo-ha!)

But The Candy Store, now that's a story all unto itself. Growing up in the Bronx the local candy store held a special meaning. It was a hang-out for all the pre-teens who might enter and buy a penny Hershey

Bar or a three cent (if you could afford that extravagance) frozen Milky Way. Or once in a while there were those long pretzels for a penny, the ones covered with salt (who heard of high blood pressure?) And now we're told that salt and pressure...but that's another column. And as we decided on our purchase we flicked through the magazines and comic books until the store owner yelled at us, "This isn't the public library."

But we were not intimidated by that first shout. After all, we had our pennies, we were bona-fide patrons, and when you're twelve, the world is your oyster. Or perhaps considering our religious orientation, the world was our white fish. (That doesn't quite make it. Oh well...)

But the candy store was a mecca of items. It was where you got Papa the daily newspaper for two cents. And then he would pass it along to Benjy, the man with the bad leg on the ground floor. Papa would tell me to bring Benjy the paper because it's hard for him to get out and money doesn't grow on trees, and why should he spend the two cents when the used paper was as good as new. And it was a real *mitzvah*. So who could argue?

And at the candy store you could get a soda, a "two cents plain," with U-Bet chocolate syrup, and if Mama was with you she would always say, "Don't be stingy with the milk. The milk makes strong bones, and who needs so much seltzer?"

And also at the candy store, Mama would buy a chocolate malted for my brother for a nickel because it would put "skin on his bones" – and so the nickel was worth it. As for me, I had enough skin on my bones and so I waited until my brother said he couldn't finish the malted from the silver aluminum dispenser, and Mama would ask for a fresh glass so that we could share.

Also the candy store had paste and Band-Aids, paper

and notebooks, and pencils and pens (that was before the advent of the ball point, so we used pen-points that you dipped into ink and if you got it on your shirt, don't ask!). And there were crayons and even some games, not many, and once in a while a plastic wind-up animal.

Every bit of space was used. Every shelf was laden with treasures, from the large glass bowls that contained the penny candy to the fountain that dispensed soda water, to the malted machines and the racks of magazines and comic books. And we gathered and looked and Old Mr. Green yelled, "Hurry up, make room. After all this isn't..." and under our breath we murmured, "the public library."

And Fat Rosie said to Tanta Pesha, "Come let's take a walk to the Dollar Store. If I keep sitting here, I'll get glued to the chair. And I know I don't need another *chatschka*, but for under-a-dollar I could give it for a gift when I go to my daughter-in-law. If I wrap it in fancy paper she'll never know the price, and in her house... But enough, let's go."

And they went.

The Automat

"Such elegance! Such a special event!"

There was a lull in the conversation. None of the ladies sitting in front of the yellow apartment house spoke. And then Fat Rosie From 3-C broke the silence.

"So tell me, what's for supper? Somebody's cooking something special maybe? Give me an idea."

Lillie With The Hair spoke up. "Who knows? The last minute I'll throw something together. When you cook for one person nothing is special. Ever since my poor Abie..." (and here there came a deep sigh and then a reverential pause from all those assembled) and then she continued, "for one person, a lamb chop with a little salad, maybe a baked potato and a green vegetable, or I'll saute some broccoli with garlic and a few tomatoes for color. *Oy*! Believe you me, when a person is alone, who feels like preparing a meal? You eat to keep up your strength but there's no enjoyment."

The other ladies nodded in agreement even though it was common knowledge that "poor Abie" had not "passed away," but had gone off with the manicurist from the neighborhood beauty salon over seven years ago.

To change the subject, Tanta Pesha said, "So maybe you all heard about what the special is at the little restaurant by the park?" Gertie didn't miss a beat, "Why should I eat out? When I eat what I make, at least

I know what's in the pot. When you eat out who knows? Now my daughter-in-law, the fancy lady who has no time to lift up a phone...but for restaurants she has plenty of time. And when I call her and ask if today she's eating in or she's eating out, I know already the answer. When she eats out, they go to a restaurant and when they eat in, they order the food to be delivered from the restaurant...a big difference."

Tillie interrupted her. "So don't complain. It's better than my daughter-in-law. Believe me a *ballabusta* she's not. I told her that maybe I should write in my will that I should be buried outside of MacDonalds, because then I would know that she'd come by a couple of times a week." There was a clucking of teeth and a nodding of heads to show that everyone understood the problems being aired.

And the talk of restaurants and eating out caused me to recall that – growing up in the Bronx and living on a strict budget – eating out in a fancy restaurant was not part of our mental vocabulary. And yet... and yet... once in a while Mama and Papa gave us a handful of nickels and I went with my brother to the Automat.

Of course, we avoided the section where hot foods were served over the counter by chefs in white aprons. We made a bee-line for the walls with little windows encasing smaller compartments. There, one could see all sorts of delicacies. And for a nickel or two (three was out of the question) that you deposited, the little windowed door would automatically (hence the name automat, aha!) open and you could extract the offering that was behind the glass enclosure.

My favorite was the little glazed cake placed on a doily on a plate. There was a choice of the chocolate or vanilla. But for me, that was no contest. The chocolate always won. And to wash down the calories, there was always a glass of cold milk. And so for two nickels, one for the cake and one for the milk, I had a special treat.

Of course, I always asked for a straw to go with the milk. And I nibbled away at the cake ever so slowly, making certain to finish each morsel and even scraping the few bits of chocolate glaze that adhered to the plate or fell off the doily. Such elegance! Such a special event! And all for the price of two nickels.

And if by some magical transmission of thought waves, Tanta Pesha smiled at the ladies around her and said, "So girls, do you remember the Automat on Burnside Avenue? You remember what you could get for a nickel?"

And Gertie forgot to tell the story of her daughter-in-law and the cleaning lady and instead remarked, "*Oy* Pesha, those were such happy days."

And Lillie With The Hair nodded in agreement. "You said a mouthful. At least then I had my poor Abie, may he... may he..." Again a reverential pause. "But then we didn't have the two nickels to spend every day. So today I got the two nickels, but I don't got..."

Pesha didn't let her finish, "Lillie, enough with the nickels. What's was, was. And what is, is. And for that be grateful. Yes? No?"

All the ladies smiled and said, "Pesha, you're a smart woman."

And who could disagree?

The Barbershop

"This was part of being allowed
into a man's world."

Tanta Pesha walked in with two bundles. I hurried to take them out of her hands, but she wouldn't allow me to assist her. "Enough, enough," she told me, "You don't have to help. An old lady I'm not, although I'm no spring chicken either." She placed the paper bags on the table before she continued.

"Such a sale they're having at the super market! You wouldn't believe. The orange juice I like with the extra vitamins and fresh squeezed is down by a dollar and the cottage cheese, the kind that's made with the skinny milk (I didn't interrupt to tell her that it was skim milk) is on sale. Such a bargain! I couldn't resist. So I treated myself to a muffin, the kind..." Here she paused and began to scrutinize me.

"Something wrong?" I asked. I could see there was but she was hesitating. I persisted. "So tell me what's the problem. I can see that you're looking at me in a funny way."

Tanta Pesha took a breath, gave a little smile, and said, "Maybe you'll tell me it's none of my business, but what's with the hair? You want maybe the barber should go out of business and his wife should go on welfare?"

I got the message. I touched my head and smoothed down my hair and said, "You're telling me I need a haircut?"

Tanta Pesha was not to be outdone. "*Dahling*, you

121

need all the hairs cut. Either that or you should begin to play the violin. And look don't go to the beauty salon with all the "sexy" haircuts. (Again I didn't tell her that the word was "unisex." No need to bring on another sermon.) Where you should go is to Max The Barber. Now *he* knows how to cut hair! And you don't need the fancy perfumes and the rinses and the fancy prices. That's where you should go. Now."

It was a royal command. So I went.

And I remembered. When I was a kid, once a month, the last Friday of the month, I went to Tony The Barber. Mama would give me a quarter and also a nickel. The quarter was to pay for the haircut and the nickel was for the tip. The Barber Shop was a male-oriented establishment. Girls did not come in. It was an unwritten law. Oh, occasionally, a mother would come in, child in tow, to instruct Tony, "Short in the back. And the hairs shouldn't stand up."

Tony would listen attentively and then as soon as the shop would become a "Men Only" refuge, he would do exactly as he was wont.

The Barber Shop was special. There were large mirrors and bottles with exotic looking liquids of various colors on the shelf. I never saw Tony use any of these liquids and I never discovered the secret of what the bottles held, but it was all part of the mystique, and I was enthralled.

There was a special regimen. Tony always asked me how I was doing in school and if I was a good boy. "You listen to your Mama? You help around the house?" I assured him that I did – after all he had the razor blade and I knew that one didn't argue with that.

And when Tony put cream on my nonexistent side burns and used the razor to trim the back, he would always ask, "So what will it be? A haircut only? Or a haircut and shave?" From my eight year old psyche, I knew that this was part of being allowed into a man's world and so I said each time I was asked, "Only a haircut. Maybe next month a shave."

And Tony would laugh and announce to all the non-existent audience, "You heard that? Next month."

And as I left the chair, my hair plastered down with all sorts of perfumed liquids, Tony would give my cheek a squeeze. I handed him the quarter and then gave him the extra nickel. Tony feigned surprise and delight and told me, "All the girls will be chasing after you now. So be careful!" (I am not sure what the "be careful" meant. After all, those days were not the nineties and I was only eight years old, but I assured Tony that I would "be most careful.")

And then as if for good measure, I was told, "Look, kiddo, you come to me Monday before school and I'll comb your hair for you so you'll look good for the teacher." And of course this was part of the ritual.

All these memories went through my mind now as Max, the gentle, kindly Max, who owns the Barber Shop and who asked me how I was and if the grandchildren were keeping me busy, snipped away and combed my hair. I almost told him that "I was a good boy and got good marks in school," but I caught myself. All I said was "Everything's fine, thank God. And you?"

Max smiled and said, "So what's the use of complaining? I make a living…"

I handed him the dollar bills (more than a quarter… but look at the price of milk) and even though I was only told to take care and stay well (no mention of coming back on Monday), I waved my hand and gave a warm smile. And as I left, all I said was, "You take care too, Tony."

I heard him call as I left, "Max – not Tony."

But I was already out of the shop and didn't bother to explain.

The Dumb Waiter

*"And from this means of garbage disposal,
we learned so much more."*

Living in an apartment house (you can call it a
tenement – whatever) in the Bronx, we had a
special avenue of communication. Telephones, we
couldn't afford, although we had a rich friend whose
Papa made a lot of money. He owned a grocery store a
few blocks away and in a real emergency we could use
their phone.

But that was only for a real emergency like when
Tanta Pesha fell because the super didn't shovel the
snow from the stoop and she was carrying all the
groceries and...STOP, already. That's for another story
and besides, the doctor said she would be all right and
next time she shouldn't walk with her head up.
Otherwise, the candy store down the block had a pay
phone and if you had a nickel you could call your friend
who lived in the East Bronx.

But each of our apartments had another way of
getting in touch with someone in the building. This was
the dumb waiter. For those of you too young to
remember, let me explain. In the kitchen, right behind
the kitchen table where I sat, was the dumb waiter.
(Everyone in the family had a place at the table when
we ate. Of course, after dinner – only we called it
supper – when the dishes had been put away – we could
then use the table for homework. This was the

forerunner of recycling, I suppose.)

But I digress. So behind my chair was an opening in the wall with a door – and this was the dumb waiter. Every night at about six o'clock, the Super (do you say "superintendent"?) would ring the buzzer and Mama would open that door, place the garbage pail on the shelf, and call down, "All right." Then the Super would pull on the ropes and the garbage pail would go down, shelves and all, to the neighbor's kitchen below us, and so on, until there was no more room. Then all the garbage would descend into the basement so that the Super could empty the pails and hoist back up the dumb waiter so that we could open the door, remove the pail, and wait for another day.

Simple. But there was even more. The dumb waiter provided us with an open line of communication. Many an evening, I heard Mama call out into the open area behind the door, "3-C, you're all right? I haven't seen you shopping." Or, "4-C, how's your husband? Any luck with the new job?"

Of course, as kids this was a great opportunity for us to establish contact. We quickly learned from our parents and called out to our friends up and down the line. "Benjy, can you come down to play? Or, "Sonny, I got a new game. You wanna see?"

It was great fun being able to talk to your friends and socialize, even for a minute or two until Mama would tell us, "Enough already, finish your milk. Don't you have any studying to do? And close the dumb waiter, there's such a draft coming into the kitchen." We obeyed naturally.

And from this means of garbage disposal, we learned so much more. As other people's left-overs paraded past, we could tell that 5-C had chicken for dinner and that 4-C had made a cake that no one ate. And then there were always the little unexpected gifts. For example Mama would give a "yoo-hoo" to Fat

Rosie From 3-C. "Yoo-hoo, Rosie. I'm putting today's newspaper on the dumb waiter. Look at page three. There's a good recipe for cold slaw." (Years later I learned it was cole slaw; but I think "cold" makes more sense. Even today.)

And Rosie would thank us for sharing. That was certainly easier than having to take the paper down or up a few flights of stairs, especially since Fat Rosie might be embarrassed because she hadn't cleaned the house, since she was always talking to neighbors when better, she should be straightening up.

There was certainly something special about the dumb waiter with its smells and sounds – and – since it allowed us to communicate. But then came the day when Mama discovered bugs. She told Papa that she saw a bug crawling out of the dumbwaiter, a malevolent little creature that had no doubt made its way from one of our neighbors who didn't keep a clean house or who didn't scrub the garbage pail (probably 2-C who spends more time doing her nails when her garbage pail is so dirty).

And so Papa had to seal up the dumb waiter and we (that "we" was really "I") had to trudge down the flight of stairs to the basement with the garbage pail and empty everything into an evil-smelling metal can.

And so the years have passed. Then there came incinerators, and then recycling, and now we're in the modern (only Mama said "modren" age) and we will never know what our neighbors had for dinner or with whom we could share the latest recipe for stewed prunes on page three.

But that's life. We can't dwell in the past. The dumb waiters are gone but the memories… and the odors… still remain.

Stayin' Cool In Summer

"Kids could get into bathing suits and dash under the cold water, screeching and yelling…"

Summer! The very word brings me back to the time when we (oh-oh, now I'm beginning to sound like Queen Victoria and using the royal "we") were kids. I'm not going to give dates because after all, I do want to protect the innocent, but suffice it to say these were the days before home air conditioners – and movie theaters – were the only places that were "air-cooled."

I remember that I used to get together with my friends and stand in front of these theaters so that when the doors opened, a whoosh of cold air would come forth and relieve us from the oppressive heat of the city blocks. But soon the manager would chase us away. Enough relief for one day. Come back tomorrow.

Those were the days when all of us pre-teens would congregate "on the stoop." So now I'll explain for those of you who are not "seasoned" enough to know what a stoop is. In front of many of the apartment (again, maybe you called them tenement) houses there were two or three steps leading into the front entrance. This was "the stoop." And it was an important part of our lives.

Sometimes the boys would get to the stoop early in the morning and claim the area as our own. We could hit a ball against the edge (this was the famous "stoop ball") or talk about the latest baseball scores and batting averages. If, however, we were late to arrive, the girls might get there first and then this became lost territory. They had their paper dolls and the cut-out clothing (whoever heard of Barbie and Ken?) and there were giggles and screeches whenever we guys approached.

I suppose we were an orthodox group because there was no mixed seating. It was either just boys or just girls. Exclusive. The legal system had not yet informed us about discriminatory practices and that there had to be a mingling of the sexes. (Sex! *Oy*! Remember, those were the days when sex was dirty and the air was clean. What a reversal!)

And then in the afternoon when the temperature began to rise and the pavement heated up, all the old ladies (that meant anyone over thirty) kept repeating the lines, "Such a hot July! What will it be in August? Don't even ask. But it's not just the heat – that I can take – it's the humidity."

So what did we do to escape the heat – and the humidity, whatever that was?

We went to the school yard. For a nickel (that's five pennies that were squirreled away) we could go into the school where there was a swimming pool in the basement. They supplied the kids with towels and also soap, because everyone had to shower before entering the heavily chlorinated water. But if one was not so fortunate to have the nickel – the required sop to Cerberus – (one day I'll explain that illusion) then there were always the showers.

This was a makeshift contraption, made up of several water hoses and rigged up to a pole in the school yard. The water was turned on periodically and kids could get into bathing suits and dash under the cold water, screeching and yelling, prancing about and showing off who was the bravest and the strongest and could endure staying the longest under the frigid water.

But the best part was that the showers were free. So no nickels (no sops) were required. Such democracy! And it lasted until 4:00 in the afternoon, when all these amusements came to a halt. Then the rich kids emerged from the pool carrying their free towels while the rest of us threw our towels from home (after all, without a nickel, you didn't get a towel) over our shoulders, and all of us, rich and poor, marched – or maybe straggled –home together.

And yet there was the camaraderie. This was summer and, who knows, tomorrow we could meet on the stoop or go to the school yard (maybe I'll get a nickel from Papa) or if all else fails, we can stand in front of the movie theater and get chased by the manager.

Life was great and summer was special! And you know what – it still is. And I mean both – life and summer.

Getting A Library Card

"All this was now mine because I could sign my name."

I was five years old and I could write my name. I had been practicing how to write my name for what seemed like weeks, although it was only a day and a half. But now I was ready. I wrote my name one last time on the piece of "practice paper" that my mother had given me and it seemed perfect. It fit on the lines and I knew that everyone – EVERYONE – would be able to read it. So I took the paper with the childish scrawl to Mama, who examined it carefully while I held my breath. And then she pronounced the words, "That's fine, just fine."

And so I got my jacket, my scarf and my wool hat and, holding Mama's hand ever so tightly, we walked the eight blocks to the Public Library. I knew the way almost blind-folded because I had rehearsed the steps in my mind each day – maybe each hour – over the past several weeks. Then we climbed the steps, pushed the heavy wooden door open, and entered.

Slowly we walked to the desk. The room was filled with complete silence and there was that special scent of books – not musty – but special – that pervaded the air. The librarian looked up, her white hair in a tight bun, and glasses resting on her nose. All she said was, "Yes?"

I thought that Mama would answer for me, but she

only joined the general silence. If I was old enough to come to the library, then I must speak for myself.

I cleared my throat. I was afraid my voice would never make it through my lips. I was practically trembling with a mixture of fear, anxiety and excitement. Finally I opened my eyes wide and spoke, "I should like a library card." I had rehearsed those words a dozen times, practicing the right inflection and the correct tone. I wanted to be audible, but I didn't want to disturb the solitude that pervaded

"And how old are you?" the librarian asked.

"Five years old," I answered. That was easy and so I added. "I was five on November twelfth." And then I continued so that there would be no doubt concerning the truthfulness of my response, "My birthday... November the twelfth."

"And can you sign your name?" I knew that question was coming. Again I was prepared.

"Oh, yes... my whole name. All of it." I didn't know if I should reveal that I had been practicing all week. I wasn't even sure if I should have brought the practice paper with me. But I had no chance to continue. The lady in the brown dress, the white hair, and the glasses on her nose held out a card and said in a voice that was not quite a command, but more than a request, "Here, child, sign your name."

I took the card and the pencil that she proffered and, my heart beating loudly (would that heart-beat cut though the silence and would I be scolded for making too much noise?), I carefully wrote my name – my entire name – in the space allotted.

And then SHE looked up, adjusted her glasses, scrutinized the signature on the card, and then... and then... like the rainbow appearing after a sudden shower, there appeared on her face just the slightest, just the hint of... but I was sure that it was there, actually there, and not just in my imagination... the trace of a smile as she said… (or was it Mama who said the words? I couldn't be sure…)"That's fine, just fine."

And the card was stamped and handed back to me. And now I could borrow books – no more than two at a time – and I must return them in two weeks or else there would be a fine – a penalty – of a penny for each book – for each day that it was overdue. And I must keep my hands clean whenever I came to the library, and I must only speak in a whisper so as not to disturb the other people, and I must never bring in food or worst of all chewing gum, and… and… and…

There were many other "ands" that I was told. But none of that mattered. I now had a library card and the world of books suddenly opened up. I looked around at all the shelves and stacks and stacks of books… and one day I would read them all. All this was now mine because I was five years old and I could sign my own name.

One day I would read Ecclesiastes (or perhaps you know the scroll by the title "Koheleth"). And there I would read, "Of piling up books there is no end…"

But did Koheleth… or Solomon… whoever…know what it was to be five and to write your name – and to have your own library card? If he did, would he have still written that verse? I am not certain, but I am certain, that one day many years ago, I did.

Moving

"And then last, but not least, there was the matter of concession. This required a bit of careful bargaining.

Isaw the look on Mama's face and I already knew that there was going to be trouble. I saw that look of determination and immediately knew that no amount of whining and pleading was going to dissuade her.

So I was prepared for the worst when she called us all into the kitchen – Papa included – and announced, "It's time to move." I knew that arguing would be useless, but I couldn't help myself. And before I could say "Let's talk about this," Mama let us know that talk was of no value. The lease was up and the landlord – that man whom I had never seen, but who brooded over the building like some kind of *meese n' shumeh* – some *evil spirit* – had decided to raise the rent three dollars more each month.

When Mama said, "Three dollars!" we all knew that whether this was a matter of principle or one of finances, we would not pay the increase.

And so Mama began scouting the neighborhood and I was given the responsibility of collecting cartons from the neighborhood stores – cartons that we would use for packing. (Crazy you have to be to give the movers fifty cents for a carton when you can go to a store and get one for free.)

But there were warnings to me as well. "You

shouldn't take a carton that's dirty or torn." And, "Make sure that there are no bugs in the carton – so maybe don't even bother asking Louis, that *grub yung* who owns the *trayfe* delicatessen. Such a dirty counter he has, not that I would ever buy from him, but I heard from the Super's wife that he uses a dirty mop. *Pheh.*"

So I made the rounds collecting cartons, and Mama (and Papa, too, when he was off from work) canvassed the neighborhood. We knew that we couldn't even think of living on the Grand Concourse, that elegant street fashioned after the Champs Elysee of Paris, because the rents there would be sky-high. And the same rang true for the elevator buildings. "A nice walk-up in a clean building. There shouldn't be roaches. Maybe an apartment one flight up." That was the banner under which Mama walked.

If you think that's easy, then you don't know Mama. There were many other requirements. Some rooms had to face front so you could look out and see the world and the morning sun could shine in. ("I wouldn't live in Fat Rosies's apartment if you paid me. All in the rear and so dark. *Finster vee drerd.* But don't repeat what I said. She's a nice lady and I wouldn't want to insult her. But…")

And the apartment house had to be near a school, and not that the children had to have dangerous crossings, but because the automobile drivers go like crazy and they don't care who they knock down.

And then last but certainly not least, there was the matter of concession. This required a bit of careful bargaining. First you indicated to the Super that you might – just might – be interested in taking the apartment, but how many month's concession would the landlord give? One month meant that you didn't pay rent the initial month since, after all, you had so many expenses with the mover; and two month's concession, no rent for two months, well that was a real find.

And that's exactly what Mama found – a two bedroom apartment on the first floor. The living room/dining room/family room (ha!) faced the front and had the fire escape, but faced the east and got the morning sun and the kitchen and small bedroom looked out on the courtyard. And that was where Papa would set up the clothes line so that Mama could hang out the wash each morning and gather it in each evening before dark.

And best of all the school, P.S. 70, was diagonally across the street, with a crossing guard, although Mama would watch from the window to make certain that we would not get run over by some *meshugeneh* driver. (How her watching could have helped us avoid the tragedy is beyond me, but Mama knew better. And I did not question.)

And so we moved. But first there was the packing and the giving away, and the throwing out, and the arguing over what should go and what should stay. Who needs the broken vase? Not so broken – only cracked a little. And what's with all the comic books – it makes for worms. And this medicine – it's still good? And each decision was punctuated with a sigh from Mama who told one and all that she hated to move. ("But Mama, it was your idea." "Don't be smart, *Dahling*, just pack.") And we packed, even in the carton that looked a little dirty. And we moved.

But there was always a bright side. Because as Tanta Pesha pointed out, "Remember. It's easier to move than to paint." And who can argue with that logic?

Giving and Getting an Honor

*"If you run from honors, honors
will run after you."*

Rosie From Apartment 3-C heaved a sigh. "Such a day! I can't believe. Not too hot, not too cold. Just perfect."

She invited Gertie With The Nails to join her in front of the empty lot where she had set up a folding chair and was enjoying the sun. "So sit down Gertie and take a load off your feet. Look here's a box that that nice Chinese lady who runs the grocery store gave me. You take it. I have my chair today."

Gertie hesitated for a minute and then corrected, "Korean." Rosie looked puzzled, "What's that you said?"

Gertie explained, "Korean. The nice Chinese lady from the grocery is Korean. And nice she is. By me, there's no argument on that account. And the children, so polite and helpful. The big boy, not even ten and he always helps me carry my groceries to my apartment. And when I wanted to give him a nickel he wouldn't take it. So I offered him some cookies, and those he took."

And with that, Gertie accepted the offer and sat down, but not before she offered a sigh of her own. "So why are you *kvetching* like that?" asked Rosie. And Gertie told her, "It's my rheumatism or my arthritis. All the bones ache. I must be getting old."

Rosie laughed, "So who isn't. Look at me. I'm no spring chicken. But you gotta make the best of it. Smile and the world smiles with you. Cry and you need a box of Kleenex." And she too heaved a philosophic sigh.

It was then that Minnie From Across The Street passed by carrying a neatly wrapped package. The ladies invited her to sit down, but Minnie declined the offer explaining that she had some errands to take care of. "So maybe when you're finished with the errands, you'll come back and *shmooze* a little. After all it's been a while since you told us about the children, especially your son the dentist who plays the flute."

Minnie smiled. "Clarinet. But it's nice you remembered."

Rosie laughed. "Remembered! How could we forget? When I had such pain that I thought my head would come off, he saw me one-two-three – and such golden hands. My whole mouth he saved. *A leben af em.* And he took my insurance and treated me like I was the Queen of England. So what if he doesn't play the flute any more. Who cares?" With a smile and a wave of the hand, Minnie was off.

Rosie said, "A nice lady. A fine person. Real genuine. (She pronounced it "gen-u-wine.") And I know where she's going, *shlepping* that package."

"So where?" Gertie asked. Rosie hesitated, but only for a minute. "Not that she'll tell you. But she takes her used clothes, and believe me, some are in mint condition, freshly washed and ironed. All neatly folded, and then she wraps them up like it's a present and she goes over to where the little benches are."

Gertie expressed surprise. "The little benches! That neighborhood I don't like to walk to. Some of the people are... you know."

Rosie reprimanded her, "They're people. Poor yes. Out of work. And some are too proud to go to The Welfare. So Minnie goes there."

Gertie was confused. "For what she goes there?"

Rosie explained. "With the package of clothes. And

she sits on the bench for a little bit and then she leaves the package. I think that once she told one of the people, 'Maybe you know someone who could use this.' But sometimes she says nothing. Just leaves and smiles. Everyone knows her. A real *gutteh neshomeh.* God bless her."

Gertie asked, "So tell me, how do you know all this?"

All Rosie answered was "I know. Believe me, I know." And she said it with such authority that Gertie did not question any further. "That's a real *mitzvah* she does. And may she be rewarded for it." She glanced heavenward and then came down to earth.

"Tell me Rosie," said Gertie, "you know so much. Look at me. All my life I do my best. And you know what the Rabbi told us on Yom Kippur: If you run from honors, honors will run after you. So how come they never catch up with me?"

Rosie thought for a moment, then admitted this was a problem and that she couldn't give a good answer.

But had they asked Tanta Pesha, she would have told Gertie, "Maybe it's because you keep looking back."

Aha!

5. Celebrating Jewish Style

The High Holidays

"Those of us without tickets ... had to use our ingenuity to enter the shul."

Mama let out a sigh, *"Oy!* The Holidays are so early this year. It seems that we just finished with Pesach not to mention Shavuos, and soon it will be the New Year"

There was no arguing with Mama or trying to tell her that we were already half past September, that school had started several weeks ago and that it was time for Rosh Hashanah and Yom Kippur to appear on the calendar. Each year it was the same, the sigh and the comment. Although, if truth must be told, once in a while there was a variation. After the sigh came the comment, *"Oy!* The Holidays are so late this year. It's soon Rosh Hashanah and before you know it Chanukah."

But early or late (it seems that the Holidays were never on time) there was a special mood in the air. For us kids, we knew that we would be off from school and that we would be getting new shoes. Sneakers were out of the question. "Ball players wear sneakers. These shoes are for *shul*, for the synagogue, for services." (It was a three-in-one situation.)

We knew that we first wore the new shoes to synagogue and then to school. It was good luck to wear something new on Shabbos or on a holiday, and new shoes qualified.

The High Holy Days were special in many ways. First of all, all of us had to be carefully dressed and groomed. And then you needed tickets to get into the synagogue. Those of us without tickets (and this means most of us kids) had to use our wits and our ingenuity to enter the *shul*. At the door of the big synagogues (like the Mt. Eden Center or Zion Temple on the Grand Concourse) there stood a guard – not an usher – and certainly not a member of the congregation. This was a tall Irish policeman (at least he looked like a policeman – all attired in a blue uniform – and at least he looked Irish – he had blond hair and a ruddy complexion.) He was there to keep out those without tickets – and it was our solemn challenge to get past and enter. We used all the time-honored ploys:

1. *I have to see my Grandma. She forgot to take her pills.*

2. *I have a message for my Grandpa. It's important.*

And all these words were accompanied with a soulful expression, designed to melt the heart of the most austere of the security officers. Did they know that all this was a ruse? Probably. But they gave us a hard time. It was all a part of the game.

"What does your Grandma look like? How tall is your Grandfather? If I let you in will you promise not to pray?" We promised. We entered. We found friends and relatives.

The men were all downstairs and the women up in the balcony. (Rabbi Wise was once asked why the men sat downstairs and the women were above in the balcony and he said it was to remind us of Psalm 8, that "man was created a little lower than the angels." (Not bad. 'Twill serve.)

We looked at the prayer books and disregarded the mock-admonition of the guard at the door. We giggled, we prayed, we laughed, we prayed, and we whispered to each other. We were admonished to be still. We were hugged by those who knew us. And then we left to continue our journey to the next synagogue and to be on our way to a new adventure and a new challenge.

The High Holy Days were wonderful, filled with new beginnings and new anticipation. My memory bank stores these vignettes and holds on most lovingly to the Bubbies and the Zaydies, the Irish (they must have been Irish) guards, and the Rebbes with the gray beards, the aroma of old books and equally old *tallisim* (Prayer shawls in case you asked) the sea of *yarmulkes* and the low murmur of prayers. The pictures remain and sharing them with you makes them become alive and vital and adds a special quality to my message.

L'shana tova tikatayvu – May you all be inscribed in the Book of Life for a happy and healthy year, a year of peace and happiness, of renewed energy, and, even a little more prosperity.

As long as I'm asking…that wouldn't hurt either.

Making a New Year's Resolution

"I'll promise not to talk."

I approached the yellow building with the awning and spotted Tanta Pesha with her cronies huddled together. "Happy New Year!" I shouted, and they responded in unison, *"L'shanah Tovah!"*

And then Fat Rosie From Apartment 3-C said, "So come over and give me a hug. For the New Year." So I did.

"And what's new?" Tanta Pesha asked, "besides the year? Maybe it'll be a good one and a healthy one for all of us. And believe me, if you don't have your health, you got nothing."

The other ladies signaled their approval with an *"Ormayn."* And Gertie With The Nails added, *"Abee gezunt.* That's what I always say."

"Not to change the subject," I said, changing the subject, "but have you all made your resolutions for the New Year? You know what the Babylonians used to resolve?"

I could see that my bit of erudition was lost and I almost wished that I could take back my words. Lillie With The Hair was not at all fazed, "The Babylonians from across the park? I never had so much to do with them. Although the old lady has no *mazel.* Both her daughters married out."

Tanta Pesha looked upset. "Both? I thought only the older one." Lillie was quick, "Both. Both married *glitzeeyanas.* I know for a fact."

And then Pesha asked, "So what did they resolve?"

I smiled and told her, "To return all agricultural implements that they had borrowed during the year."

Gertie was the next to offer. "And well they should. Some people borrow and hold so long that they begin to feel that it belongs to them already, yet."

I must have looked a bit confused, what with the mixed marriage between *Litvaks* and *glitzeeyanas* and the Babylonians on the other side of the park. What park?

But Lillie interrupted my confusion. "I made a resolution. From now on, no gossiping. I won't be like the one from the top floor, a regular *yenta tallabenta*. All she knows is to talk on the telephone and her apartment is a regular *shmutz*. If only she took out a dust mop once in a while. *Pheh.*"

And Gertie said, "Me, I'll go to *shul* even when there's no *kiddush* after services. But if there is a *kiddush*, what will it hurt if I take a little? After all, first there's food for the soul and then...you need a little something to keep up your strength. Yes? No?"

Tanta Pesha assured her, "Of course, yes." Gertie breathed a sigh of relief and then it was Fat Rosies's turn.

"Me? Let me see. I won't talk about food or religion since you already mentioned that. But maybe if it's all right, I'll promise not to talk about my daughter-in-law, the one from Connecticut, God forbid she should pick up the phone to see if I'm alive or dead, and once in a blue moon maybe she'll remember to send me a birthday card. I won't say a bad word about her. But believe me, she should thank her lucky stars that she found a husband like my son who holds down a steady job and doesn't drink or gamble like some people I know. And I won't mention initials or names, but if you ask me how her brother is doing I just might tell you."

Tanta Pesha couldn't help but smile. "You mean you'll go a whole year without saying a bad word?"

Rosie looked up. "From my mouth will only come nice things... like, The Rabbi, he should only live to be a hundred and twenty. That beautiful Rabbi Aarontchik told us last week we must protect ourselves against a bad tongue. He called it *lashon rah*. And I believe what he said. If only my sister in Manhattan listened to him, she would never spread such terrible stories. But that lazy husband of hers doesn't say a word to help her and all she does is watch television and eat take-out. You'd think that the kitchen was off limits. When she told me that she has gone around the world twice, I told her that maybe she should walk into the kitchen. That's a place I bet she's never been."

And then I looked at Tanta Pesha who only said, "Me, I'll try to be a little better than last year, which won't be hard. And if not better, then at least not worse. And meanwhile, a good year to all."

And she gave me a special hug – which I pass along to all of you.

Mama Loved Succos

*"Oy, such a sweet taste ... I can become
a regular Shikkur."*

"It's like a gift, a real *matanah* that God gives to us."
(And here Mama used the Yiddish – or was it Hebrew
expression – whatever).

And when I asked her what the gift was, she looked
at me with a semi-surprised expression that came over
a cherubic face and explained, "Why, the holidays.
What else?"

Somehow Mama regarded the holidays, each *Yom
Tov* as a special gift divinely given to her, a gift that she
was very willing to share with all the members of her
family. Even *Pesach*, which she called a 'hard holiday'
because it entailed changes of dishes and scrubbing and
washing and cleaning and preparing, even *Pesach* was
a gift that she cherished.

But I think the holiday that was her favorite was
Sukkot. (Of course she pronounced it *Succos* using the
Eastern European dialect that was so *haimish* to her,
and indeed to all of us.)

When the High Holy Days came, there was almost a
note of happy anticipation in the air because we all
knew – or at least Mama told us more than a zillion
times – that *Succos* was on the way.

Now, all the holidays held special significance for us
kids. *Rosh Hashanah* meant honey cake and *taiglach*,
that sweet honeyed delicacy with candied citrons and

raisins and nuts (is your mouth watering yet? Mine is). And *Simchas Torah* meant flags with blue and white stripes and the *Mogen David*, the Jewish Star, blazoned in the middle, and on top of the stick, an apple. And there was *Shmini Atzeres*, which we never fully understood as kids, but we loved the sound of it so much that we used to say, "I'll see you half past Shmini Atzeres." Or, "If you don't hurry, you'll be late for Shmini Atzeres," And then we would all giggle at some undefined bit of humor.

But Mama loved *Succos*. She loved the idea of going with the children to the *sukkah* behind the big *shul* on Mount Eden Avenue. Then we would all sit down on the wooden benches around the table and the Rabbi would offer us some sponge cake and even a small paper cup with wine and we all said the special blessing and Mama, who usually never touched wine except on a special occasion, a *yom tov* or a *simcha* of some sort would sip the wine and pronounce the approbation, "Delicious." And sometimes she'd add, "*Oy* such a sweet taste... I can become a regular *shikkur*." Again we would all laugh because we knew she was only fooling.

And for days after, even when the holiday of *Succos* was only a memory, Mama used to remind us what a wonderful day it was, how good the sponge cake tasted, how sweet the wine was, and what a *mitzvah* it was to be able to sit in the *sukkah* behind the big *shul*.

But that was long ago. Because, you see, when Mama was nearing her ninety-sixth birthday, her strength began to wane. And so it was that when the High Holidays approached, she prayed with a special fervor, but not with the same strength that she had when I was a child.

And when *Yom Kippur* was over and I asked Mama how she was, she informed me that she had confessed her sins (Sins! What sins?) and that she had come to terms.

Usually she said that she had made her peace, but this year the response was changed somewhat and I have to admit that I was not so happy with the change.

And so it was that a few days later Mama was taken to the hospital and never returned. For it was immediately before the holiday of *Succos* (Yes, *Succos* and not *Sukkot*) that she died and the *Yom Tov* interrupted the traditional *shivah* period of mourning.

And the next day I visited the big *shul* on Mount Eden Avenue for the last time. And Tanta Pesha and I walked in together and I sat down on one of the long wooden benches. And I became aware that Tanta Pesha did not sit down next to me, but left some space as if... as if...

I looked at that kind old lady and wanted to tell her that there would always be an empty setting whenever I sat in a *sukkah*, even if every seat was taken. And as if she guessed what my unsaid words were, she said softly, "Maybe she's in a better place, in another *sukkah*."

And all I could say was, "Maybe. Who knows? Perhaps... Perhaps..."

Chanukah and The Great Latke Debate

"So she served latkes with apple sauce and he thought the tradition argued for sour cream..."

Chanukah is coming – take out the menorah! Make sure it is polished and shiny. After all it has been in the closet, on the shelf above where you keep the Passover trays, for almost a year now. Make certain you have a full box of candles, all different colors. (Oh, some of you are telling me that you have an electric menorah that lights up automatically and works on a timer, and also plays Ha-Tikvah) and maybe you even have a dreidel or two to take down for when the children come over. What fun!

And I can remember other Chanukahs when I was young and I remember, too, a Chanukah in Israel when everywhere, in every window, there was a *chanukiah*, a menorah, with candles burning so bright that it seemed that there were a thousand fireflies in Jerusalem. And the grandchildren went from hotel to hotel, picking up treats in the lobby, mostly apple juice and *sufganiot*, – doughnuts – and "Zaydie, zaydie it's all for free. Even the guys on the street corners are giving away *sufganiot*. Here Grandpa I got one for you. Grandma won't eat it because it's got too much cholesta-cake, but I know you will."

That was a special Chanukah, but it's not far enough

back in the memory.

The Chanukah that I remember most was the one that centered about the great Latke Debate and that took place when I was very, very young. That was when there were no electric menorahs and all the Chanukah candles were orange and the little chanukiah was made of yellow metal and each night you had to scrape the orange wax from the base so that the next night we could put in new candles, one more, and we could all sing *Ma-oz tzur* or maybe *Me y'malel* or if you visited in my wife's home when she was a little red haired youngster, the song was "*Oy Chanukah, oy Chanukah, a yom tov a freilach!*"

But no musical menorah – just our voices – all in a different key. And there were no *sufganiot*, no doughnuts, with or without cholesterol (maybe there was no cholesterol! How could there be when on the first night of Chanukah there were latkes and latkes and more latkes swimming in oil.) and there were no ceramic dreidels, or porcelain dreidels, or dreidels so beautiful that the artist signed his name. But what there was was a little wooden dreidel with the letters Nun, Gimel, Hay, Shin and we could spin it and gamble away our Chanukah *gelt*, a batch of shiny pennies (no other gifts, just pennies) and if the dreidel spun well and landed on the gimel, wow, that meant you won. The shin was to be avoided because then you had to pay a forfeit which was worse than the Nun, the neutral letter, which indicated that you neither won nor lost. Oh, yes, the hay, that was a half-win, not too bad. And in the midst of all these festivities came the great latke debate.

Mama came from Russia when she was three and Papa came from Budapest when he was five. She was a *Litvak* and he a *Glitziyana*, a mixed marriage, but one that held together for a little more than fifty years. So she served latkes with apple sauce and he thought that the tradition argued for sour cream as the accompaniment. And each Chanukah as Papa ate his latkes (and even asked for a second helping) with apple sauce, I could hear him mutter under his breath, "With sour cream would be better." And Mama gave him another helping and smiled sweetly, asking "More apple sauce? Fresh, I just made it. And the apples are so sweet. I never add sugar." And each year the debate continued with Tanta Pesha siding with Mama (who else?) and Fat Rosie From Apartment 3-C saying, "I don't want to inter-mish, but I know in my house, if you'll pardon my telling you, it was sour cream."

And so today, as we recite the prayers, and light the candles, and sing the songs and the grandchildren all gather around tearing the gift wrap from the boxes, I think that, if I close my eyes and listen very carefully, today even as I wish all of you, my dear readers and friends a happy Chanukah, may all your candles burn bright and may your dreidels always land on the gimel, today with my eyes shut, I can hear her saying, "Apple sauce," and him answering, quietly but firmly, "Sour cream."

And although we serve apple sauce with our latkes, as our good Rabbi would say, "Still, on the other hand..."

The Great Purim Debate

*"Which is the most important Jewish delicacy –
the latke or hamantaschen?"*

As Tanta Pesha so often repeated, "Two Jews, three opinions." And then she would go on to tell her favorite story that the Good Lord in His Infinite Wisdom (so many capital letters!) created Rabbis (again a capital) for this reason.

For, once there was a man and wife who had a dispute which they could not settle, so, of course, they went to their rabbi (this time, no capital) and first the wife presented her point of view. And the rabbi, after listening carefully, replied, "Madame, you are absolutely right."

But now her husband had his chance and he pleaded his case. And then the rabbi stated, "Sir, you are definitely right."

The rebbitzen listened to her husband as she sat nearby and thoroughly confused, she spoke up, "Husband mine, how is it that first you told the wife she was right and now you tell her husband that he is right. They both can't be right."

The rabbi pondered for a moment and then said, "You know what. You're right too."

Such is our tradition. That's why we have the School of Hillel and the School of Shammai, each sage taking different points of view. And that is why Tanta Pesha (and me too!) can never understand those who start their conversation with, "All you Jews are always..." But Tanta Pesha always calms me down and dismisses the speaker with one word, "Anti-semeets. What can you expect?"

And so it is no surprise that we have so many debates. You all remember (and in case you don't, why don't you?) the great Latke Debate that took place every year in my home, over – which is to be preferred as an accompaniment to the potato latke – sour cream or apple sauce? (I know this one must still be going on whenever the month of Kislev appears on the calendar).

But now we are in the month of Adar and with Purim right around the corner there comes another Debate. (This absolutely requires a capital letter.) This discussion occupies the scholar's mind in Hillels from the University of Chicago to Brandeis from the West Coast to the East, North, and South, and on many college campuses. And if it hasn't reached your neighborhood college yet, don't worry it will. So now I'm alerting you to the question on hand: Which is the more important Jewish delicacy in our tradition – the Latke or the Hamantasch?

Now this is *takkeh* a dilemma. So all the great minds, all the Rabbinical authorities, all the academic scholars met and debated, debated and argued, argued and discussed. Such a commotion! Such a yelling and screaming! Everyone tried to put aside the differences that separated each other. The Orthodox spoke to the Reform; the Lubavitch sat down with the Reconstructionists; the Conservatives listened to the Hassidim. For once there was *sholem* in the Jewish community.

The President of the Hillel organization spoke up. "It is as if the Messiah is here. Now there remains only one problem to be resolved, so let us vote: will it be the Hamantasch or the Latke?"

Immediate hands went up. "Are the latkes made with

coarsely grated potatoes?" Another hand, "The Hamantasch are prune or poppy or apricot?"

"What does it matter?" called the Hillel contingent.

"*Narashkeit.* Of course it matters," yelled the Shammai representatives.

"Let's vote first and discuss later," called the Conservatives.

"Discuss, then vote," called the representative from Hadassah.

And once again there was a *geshrai* followed by a *gevalt.* And there was such a *broo-ha-ha* that one could almost sense amidst all the noise and the points of order and the exclamations that the Messiah, if indeed he was nearby, was slipping away. But there was more wrangling and more debating and everybody was expressing an opinion in this great and portentous debate.

And as far as I know, the vote was never taken, and the discussion goes on, even today. Even today during the month of Adar, but who cares? It's Purim. So rejoice and be happy.

Passover – No Longer the Lenten Season of Deprivation

"There's even bagel mixes and pancake mixes and pizza!"

Purim is hardly a memory and already everyone is talking Pesach. Not Passover, mind you, but Pesach. What's the difference, you may ask? So I'll tell you – or better yet, let me quote Mama.

"Passover is for the modren folk," (and, no, I didn't misspell 'modern') for the those who lived on the West Side."

In The Bronx (so who remembers The Bronx, raise your hand. Come on admit it. You'll get extra credit.) the Grand Concourse was the Great Divide between the East and the West. The Fancy Folk lived on – you guessed it – the West Side; and they were the ones who spoke of Passover. We spoke of *Pesach.*

So *Purim* was put away and the taste of hamantaschen, the sound of the *groggers* were all but a pleasant memory. Already the wicked Haman was to be replaced by the cruel Pharaoh and the *hamantaschen* spot would be taken by macaroons. So why is it that every Jewish holiday always has its share of villains and cookies?

But for us kids, all we sensed was a feeling of frenzy. Cartons of eggs filled the living room. So many eggs! No one knew about cholesterol — they would never be able to pronounce it let alone spell it. And there were stacks of raisins that were needed for the wine. Who ever heard of Kedem or Mogen David wine (except for the amulet around your neck) or store-bought bottles?

And Mama had to prepare the beets and talk about the new *gefilte fish* recipe.

And the cleaning – so much cleaning. Dishes emerged from closets that had not been opened for eleven months. And then from cartons there emerged pots and pans, cutlery, and table linen, all of which we greeted like old friends or *mishpacha* ("family" for my "modern" friends) that suddenly reappeared every spring. And all had to be scrubbed and washed and dried and covered. Just in case you're thinking "dishwasher," stop.

And then all the clothing had to be inspected and pockets emptied just in case a crumb of forbidden *chometz* had secreted itself away and might wait, lurking in a secret place. (But who in the world would want to eat a morsel of stale rye bread during the days of *Pesach?* Who? Better not to ask.)

And so more scrubbing and more washing and more cleaning before the real work began – preparing for the elaborate Seder. And there were no words of complaint, no moans and groans – well, maybe a few "*oyz*" and an occasional "*oy vay*" that slipped past. Well, after all, we're all entitled. Didn't the Israelites whine a wee bit under the heavy load of their taskmasters?

They tell the story of a Jew who decided to be very "modern" – so much in fact that he decided that he wanted to emulate his Christian neighbors – and so he converted. He explained to his wife that it would be good for their social life and even his business would improve. His patient wife listened to all his rationale and then asked, "So why couldn't you convert before *Pesach?*" (Somehow Mama didn't laugh; she only gave one of her sighs and a tiny *"oy vay."*)

But that was then and this is now. And so we return to the present. Now we have dishwashers and vacuum cleaners and even dust busters to get into those little crannies where crumbs of stale rye bread might seek to take refuge. No longer is *Pesach* the Lenten season of deprivation that it used to be. Why – the supermarket shelves are stocked with all sorts of holiday goodies. Our children have begun to believe that all gefilte fish comes in bottles (no longer do they savor the aroma of fresh pike being ground and rolled with an onion added to make both the eyes and palate water).

And wine – why, wine comes in bottles, neatly stacked in the neighborhood liquor store. (Forget the raisins!) And now there's chocolate chip macaroons and mocha swirl and coconut delight and Viennese treat and there's ice cream and chocolates and cakes of all sorts and chocolate covered matzos and thin mints and gourmet nuts and herring in jars and... I can't stop, but I'm out of breath. You fill in the rest. There's even bagel mixes and pancake mixes and dry cereals and pizza (honest-to-*Pesach*, that too) – so here I go again.

And it is the spring time of the year and the green buds begin to come forth. Our children will sing of the march to freedom and they will rejoice as they tell of redemption. But we hope, too, they will give a moment's thought to those who are still in slavery, chained to poverty, to illiteracy, to ignorance, to bigotry, to a lack of knowledge of our glorious and still evolving history.

Enough of such seriousness. *Dayenu*! Now it is time to sing of the little goat and to search for the special *afikoman*, the matzo that has been secreted and saved for dessert. And it is time, too, for me to wish all of you, *"A zissen Pesach! – A very sweet and happy holiday!"*

Wedding Plans

*"A wedding without chopped liver is one thing,
but no soup or kugel – this is unheard of."*

L illie With The Nails was so excited she could hardly contain herself. "What a weekend I had. If I live to be as old as Macushla, I'll never forget it. Don't ask."

"So what happened?" Gertie With The Hair asked. "Tell us already. All day we haven't got."

All the Ladies were curious by now. And so Lillie sat down on the park bench, took a deep breath, and began. "You remember my cousin Sara Without The "H" – you know the *Greener Couziner...*"

There was a five second pause giving everyone time to acknowledge that indeed they remembered. "Well," Lillie went on, "her daughter, Mindy, the one with the big mouth, such a *pisk*, well you won't believe it but she got married!"

Tanta Pesha was the only one who did not express surprise. "So why not? For every cup there's a saucer."

But Lillie stopped her. "But we all thought she missed her chance already. After all, she's no spring chicken. Thirty she'll never see again, believe me and no matter how many times you go to the beauty parlor, you can't hide all the lines and – how many times she has her hair streaked. But that's water over the bridge. She found this nice boy from Brooklyn, with a steady job, and now poof. But for a while it was touch and miss."

Gertie became curious. "So how?" And so the story went on.

"First her Mama cried and told everyone that she's losing a daughter, until we explained that she was gaining a closet, so how bad could that be? Then she complained that they were going to move to New Jersey, over the bridge, a regular wilderness, until we told her that there was a bus you could take and there were big supermarkets and even kosher butchers in New Jersey. So that was settled. But then came the real problem."

Tanta Pesha took a guess. "Mindy opened her mouth? I know that that girl has a regular mouthpiece that the whole army could fall into if she's not careful."

But Lillie assured the Ladies that it was not Mindy – it was the groom. "First he wanted the photographer shouldn't take fancy pictures – just a few snapshots – and when the photographer came with boxes and chairs, with flags and curtains for a backdrop, the groom gave a *geshrai* – 'So where are the whips and chains?' And we all thought that he was going to have a stroke!"

Tanta Pesha asked, "Who the groom, or the photographer?"

But Lillie was not to be put off and simply said, "Whatever." But then came the terrible part. It seemed that the two of them wanted special food, strictly vegetarian, with pasta for the main course and no *kugel,* only red potatoes – and you wouldn't believe when I tell you. They said absolutely, positively no soup. So the caterer said, 'A wedding without chopped liver is one thing, but no soup and no *kugel* – this is unheard of. All the guests will complain.'"

And I'm told that Mindy With The Big Mouth said, "So let them complain. It's my wedding!"

"*Oy,*" continued Lillie, "no wonder she found the boy from Brooklyn, like two peas in a *knish.* I'm told they insisted so that the caterer promised to do whatever they wanted. So that's the story."

By now everyone was holding their breath until Tanta Pesha broke the silence. "So fast tell us before we all have a heart attack. They got married? Yes? No?"

Lillie would not allow the story to reach its conclusion so quickly, so she smiled a smile, clasped her hands in a prayerful manner and then announced, "So I'll tell you. They got married, yes, and they are going to move not to New Jersey, but all the way north to White Plains, and who knows if even they have a bus that goes. And what's more..."

Tanta Pesha looked up, "There's more?"

Lillie gave a triumphant smile, "There's always more. You know what, the soup was delicious, only a little too salty. But the *kugel* was out of this world and even Mindy With The Mouth had to agree – and the big shot from Brooklyn ate three pieces. But who's counting?"

Birthdays Are Special

"Now as far as Mama was concerned, she never wanted anyone to make a big fuss over her 'day.'"

I know that T.S. Elliot (I'm showing off now so be careful) said that April was the cruelest month, but for me April was a month of birthdays. My big brother had his birthday in April (and I suppose he still has, since some things do remain the same) and my Uncle Max (the good uncle who lived in Memphis with Elvis Presley... well actually he lived with my Aunt Sylvia, but you get the general idea). And according to tradition, Willie Shakespeare (there I go showing off again) had his family sing "Happy Birthday" to him on April 23rd.

And especially there was Mama. Her birthday was April 15 (this was before the IRS decided to make this day one to remember. Believe me, Mama came first. And in more ways than one.) And so now we have another birthday.

The *Jewish Times* is celebrating its first year this month. So April is really very special!

Now as far as Mama was concerned, she never wanted anyone to make a big fuss over her "day."

"Let every day be special," she told us. And we only half believed her. As far as we were concerned (and here I may be using the "royal we" when I really mean I) birthdays meant presents and cake and even ice cream, if you're lucky.

But Mama insisted that she didn't need more *chatchkas* or *nik-noks* to dust and I could never think of going into the "lady's section" of a store to buy an article of clothing. I wouldn't even know the right size, so I contented myself with making a card (The store-bought cards were at least five cents and early in life I was taught the value of frivolous spending.) and I didn't even ask how to spell words. "Love" I knew and "Happy" was easy – and so what if I wrote "Happy Bird-day?" The message was clear and it lost a good deal in the translation.

And so when April 15 came by, I could hardly wait to place my card on the kitchen table so that when Mama came in, she could pick it up and be so surprised and shout, "What's this? A letter? I didn't know that the mail came so early. Look, a card, for ME! I wonder who could be sending me a card?"

And then we would shout, "Happy Birthday!" And there would be hugs and kisses all around. Even Papa. And he hardly ever kissed Mama in front of us kids, although I remember once … but that's not for this story.

And I remember that Papa once bought cup cakes for dessert (and even a few Yankee Doodles, with the cream on the inside) and I even said could we light candles, but Mama said "No" – that it would be a fire hazard because of all the flames – and we all laughed because we knew that it was a joke, even if we couldn't understand the point.

But no matter how Mama played it down, birthdays are still very special to me.

And now that April is here and my very favorite newspaper (even more favorite than the *New York Times*) is having its birthday, I think that we should all take some time out to wish all the boys and girls on the staff and also Shy Kramer, who is one great guy (and if you don't take my word, just ask Tanta Pesha), "*Mazel Tov*."

Because without them, there would be no Tanta Pesha, no Fat Rosie From 3-C, and, who would think of Mama and Papa, and Uncle Max, and Gertie With The Nails or Lillie With The Hair, or the Lady with the Jewish husband, and the yellow apartment house in the Bronx, or the walk up with the dumb waiter and the clothes line? All those memories would just be gathering dust.

So as Mama would say, "Presents we don't need but … on the other hand, more subscribers and more advertisers (go to your neighborhood stores and nudge, nudge, nudge) that wouldn't hurt, believe you me. So again a Happy Birthday and who needs ice cream and cake? Unless, of course, it's chocolate.

6. School – More Than An Education

Third Grade — Eraser Monitor and Crushed Feelings

"I was afraid to look at Miss Goldman to see if she was laughing."

When I entered third grade at P.S. 70 in the Bronx, I was quite excited. This was a new year, a new teacher and new and exciting adventures. And that first week two experiences took place that have stayed with me all these years.

First of all, our teacher, Miss Goldman, announced that every child would be given a job, a responsibility. She then told us of the various jobs that would be assigned.

There was the Plant Monitor who took charge of the two snake plants (this job I did not opt for since I had a brown thumb – anything I touched invariably withered and passed on). There was the Monitor of the Goldfish bowl (here again, I did not volunteer – who wanted to be responsible for another living thing and hold life and death in your hands?) And then there was the very coveted Monitor of the Chalkboard Erasers.

Now this was a job I would have given my dessert for. Every day that envied child would gather up the erasers from the blackboard and carry them down to the yard where they would be beaten against the wall so that the excess chalk dust (now that's a good phrase, chalk dust. Hmmm, perhaps one day that image…who knows?) from the erasers would be dissipated.

Well, when that job was announced, my hand went up as high as I could stretch. And then wonder of wonders, miracle of miracles, I was chosen. I had won the coveted prize and I felt then that life could not be any more wonderful.

I looked at Miss Goldman with such gratitude and such affection and she smiled back at me and then went on to choose Paul to be the Attendance Monitor. And so I felt that life was perfect in the third grade, little knowing that every silver lining has a cloud and that the brilliant sun of my happiness would soon be hidden by that cloud. And so it happened.

It was a Friday. The last day of the school week. I went down to the school yard with my two board erasers in hand and began to pummel them against the designated wall. I wanted them to be clean, nay, cleaner than clean, for the lovely and wonderful Miss Goldman would soon be using them to erase the board before the weekend and I didn't want to have her hands soiled with the dust.

So there I was, this rather chubby cherub (alliterative, eh?) carrying these two erasers and walking across the schoolyard where all the boys and girls of the third and fourth grade had assembled to enter the building following lunch time. And there was Miss Goldman talking to the teacher of the fourth grade, Miss Spinet, she with the long pointy nose and the thin lips.

As I passed by, she stopped her conversation and fixed me with a stare that was neither friendly nor hostile and then with a smirk she told me to take out the books that I had under my sweater.

I had no books under my sweater. And so I looked up without understanding while she repeated, "Take out those books under your sweater. Surely that can't be all you."

I didn't understand. It was all me. There were no books. And then all the boys and girls began to laugh. I turned beet red. Miss Goldman wasn't laughing and neither was Gloria who sat behind me in the third row. And then Miss Spinet feigned an apologetic embarrassment and told me, "Oh, I'm so sorry. I thought that there was extra padding under your sweater. Maybe you should begin to skip desserts after lunch."

And then even Gloria began to giggle and I felt my eyes begin to water and I said over and over again to myself, "Don't cry. Don't cry." I even tried to smile and pretend I saw the joke, but I knew that I was the victim of the humor and so the smile would not appear, but neither did the tears – at least not outwardly. I was afraid to look at Miss Goldman to see if she was laughing. What if she was?

But like the tongue that seeks the aching tooth, I forced myself to meet my teacher's gaze, and all I saw was that same kind and gentle expression. And she said, "Thank you for such a good job with the board erasers."

When Monday came, the whole incident was forgotten. Gloria never said a word and neither did Miss Goldman and even when I passed Miss Spinet in the corridor she seemed to look right through me as if I didn't exist. But I remembered – and to this day I sometimes ask myself why educated people could be so unthinking and cause such unhappiness to a third grade child who only wanted to keep the board erasers clean.

Test Day and Demons

"And then it happened. Lulu gagged and threw up."

I'm remembering back to those days when I was in elementary school (no age comments, please) and on Friday it was "Test Day." And when I say Test, I mean white paper test. So understand that whenever the teacher quizzed us during the week, yellow paper was handed out to each of the children. But on Friday, this was special, and so we were all given white paper and with the change of color came a change of attitude.

And what a change. I remember Lulu Stitts. In third grade she was eight years old, going on nine. Lulu was a charming little girl who came to school in carefully fashioned braids and a well starched dress. She was friendly to everyone and she even talked to the boys at recess.

But on Friday a terrible change came over her. No sooner did the teacher take out the white paper and announce that there was going to be a spelling test or an arithmetic quiz, then a change came over Lulu. The rosy cheeks faded into a white pallor. And suddenly there came some strange sounds from Lulu. Her eyes clouded over and began to fill with tears. Her hands trembled as she stared at the teacher holding the white paper.

And then...and then...it happened. Lulu gagged and threw up. All over the desk. All over the books. All over her starched dress. All over her hands – her hands that a minute ago were perspiring and clasping a pencil as tight as possible. We all stared. No one spoke. The only movement was Miss Reilly, the teacher, rushing to summon the custodian who arrived minutes later with broom and pail and sawdust. Loads of sawdust.

Poor Lulu. I remember the look on her face as she left the room to go who-knows-where to wait for her mother to come so that she could go home, change, and wash up. Even when she returned to class a while later, she was the object of all our scrutiny.

And then the following week on Friday out came the white paper and a repeat of the same scenario. After several weeks, we all came to know what to expect and all of us pleaded not to sit too close to Lulu, until finally Miss Reilly got the message and Lulu became an Eraser Monitor and was allowed to take the board erasers into the school yard to bang them against the wall so that the excess chalk could be removed. This job was always carried out right before the white paper test took place.

We never learned if Lulu ever took those tests or if she ever stopped throwing up, because Lulu left the third grade a few months into the school year and someone else became the Eraser Monitor. I think it was Paul, the kid who stuttered – but I can't guarantee that.

And so why do I dredge this memory up from the recesses of my remembrance bank? I think partly it is because once in a while I remember Lulu Stitts. She is no longer eight going on nine. Perhaps she is married with children and even grandchildren. And those children no doubt have gone to third grade.

I wonder if there are still "white paper tests" that terrify young children. I wonder if there are still custodians who come to classrooms, armed with sawdust and pails. I wonder if there are still Miss Reillys who take weeks before they realize that somewhere in their classroom there sits a Lulu Stitts who four days a week is sweet and charming and who talks to the boys at recess. But on the fifth day when it's Friday and the white paper appears...

But I remember too that Miss Reilly finally made Lulu the Eraser Monitor and perhaps this was almost as good as a fifty minute session with the neighborhood shrink. (And perhaps not.)

But most of all I keep hoping that Lulu and all the other Lulus who are in third grade will not be terrified by a piece of paper. Even if it's white.

And yet I know full well that there are other demons waiting to abuse our children. And perhaps they are not all so easily solved by moving away, or becoming a monitor, or leaving the room when the test begins...

Learning How To Save Money

*"I came to school on Monday to put a dime
in the bank envelope and when I looked
into my pocket – no dime."*

I was eight years old and ready to enter the world of high finance. It was a Monday morning and here I was in the second grade at P.S. 7 in the Bronx. Our teacher, Mrs. Arak, told us to clear our desks and clasp our hands on top of the desk. She stared long and hard at Paul who was fidgeting with his pencil – until under the chill of her glance he stopped. I think that I stopped breathing.

And then Mrs. Arak took out of her desk drawer a group of little wax envelopes. "Today, boys and girls, you are going to learn how to save money," she announced.

I thought that I already knew how to save money. You put it in the little china sugar bowl with the chip on it that Mama kept in the kitchen near the cereal set. At least I was certain that's where Mama used to put the extra money that was left over at the end of the week after all the bills were paid. She always told my brother and me, "It's important that you save something at the end of every week so that you come out ahead."

Of course, these were the days before credit cards – and buying on the installment plan was definitely a no-no in our home. Even though money was tight – that was never a real cause for arguments in our home. That doesn't mean that Papa never complained that Mama didn't spend enough on herself – but that she was always putting away the "extra."

"What do I need another dress? For what?" she asked. "I only have one back. But for a man it's different. You have to dress presentable because you go out into the world and it's important to make a good appearance. End of case. Period."

And so the argument stopped before it had a chance to begin. And Mama squirreled a little more away into the chipped china bowl.

So now it was that I told everyone that I was going to open up my own bank account, and that each Monday we would get a little envelope and we could put some coins (no pennies, just silver. And bills were…well, let's be real…we weren't millionaires like Rockefeller) into this envelope and our bank accounts would grow and grow.

This was so exciting and I was given a nickel each week to deposit. And there were even some special weeks, like Chanukah time or my birthday that I was handed a dime! And whenever my Uncle Max from Memphis came to visit, he would give me a whole batch of quarters (maybe even five or six!) and so for weeks that bank account was fortified.

I even remember that I earned four cents interest, extra money for doing nothing. Just for banking! Life was so glorious! I almost forgot that we were living in bad times, that Mama walked four extra blocks to go to the new market where oranges were a penny cheaper if you bought three and that they sold you day-old rolls for half price. So who cared? If you put the rolls in the oven it was just fine.

But for Papa it was different. He got a fresh roll each morning because as Mama philosophized, "A man has to keep up his strength," and Mama told him that she liked the rolls to be a little hard (was that another way for saying "stale?") because she felt that fresh rolls were hard for her to digest and the day-old rolls had fewer calories. (Don't ask me to explain that one.)

And so – picture the day that I came to school on Monday to put a dime in the bank envelope and when I looked in my pocket – no dime – an empty pocket. I was devastated. I couldn't wait to get home and search my room…every room. I was trembling and I didn't want to tell my Mama that I had lost my money. I looked all over – but all in vain. I knew that I had to tell.

What would Mama do? How could I be so careless? I knew she wouldn't yell or scold (and certainly not hit), but she would give me a look and that would be punishment enough.

So first, before I faced the real music, I whispered to Papa what had happened. He didn't say a word. He could be so quiet. And as we sat down for dinner (supper?) I announced that I had something to say.

But before I could confess my sin…my crime…my carelessness, Papa said in the softest voice I heard, "I found a dime on the kitchen floor. I think you dropped your bank money."

And he gave me the coin. I hugged him and felt tears on my cheek, but I was not certain if they were mine or his, and I hardly heard Mama warning me to be more careful with money because "it doesn't grow on trees."

Papa didn't say a word and neither did I. I knew that next Monday I would deposit a dime in my bank account.

And I wondered just for a very little bit how it was that Papa had found my lost dime when I was so certain that it was two nickels that I had brought with me that morning.

Not Being Chosen

"I laughed and told Little Billy that we had a special position – 'left out.'"

I never knew his real name. Everyone called him Buddy. Our fourth grade teacher Miss Halpern called him Buddy. All of the boys and girls in the school called him Buddy. His big brother Paul called him Buddy. I suppose that his mother and father called him Buddy, but I never heard them call him anything.

Buddy wasn't in my class. He was in the "2" class and I was in the "1" class. Now in the school that I attended, P.S. 70 in the Bronx, children were placed in classes according to their teacher's assessment of their academic ability.

The "1" class was for the brightest (ha!) kids. Then came the "3" class, then the "4" class, and at the very bottom – the lowest rung on the intellectual ladder – was the "2" class. And that was where Buddy was placed.

Those who knew him and were unkind called him "stupid" – of course, this was said when Buddy wasn't nearby. Others who were gentler termed him "slow." All I knew when I was ten years old and in the fourth grade, was that Buddy was almost twelve; that he had been "left back" at least once or maybe twice; that he was at least two heads taller than I; and that even though he couldn't do long division, when it came to baseball, he was the best hitter in the fourth grade – or maybe in the whole school – or even the world!

And I also knew – oh how well I knew – that while I was terrific with spelling and arithmetic and "A#1" in reading, I was the last to be chosen when the fourth grade met for gym in the outside yard. Even Little Billy who used to giggle and who never seemed to be able to walk straight was always picked by the team captains right before me.

Oh, once in a while, I noticed a sense of hesitation when the two last kids to be chosen were Billy and I. And then with a sigh, the finger pointed to Billy and the captain said, "I'll take *him*."

And now two incidents come to mind. I'm not one hundred percent certain which came first but both happened during that year in the fourth grade, and I like to think – oh, how I like to think – that the spelling bee came first.

We had four teams and we all met, the whole fourth grade, in the auditorium. Each team had a captain and I was chosen to lead the Golden Warriors. Each captain could choose his team members – five to a team. And we would work as a team to decide on the spelling of each word – a group effort. Everyone wanted to be chosen and all my friends tried to capture my attention.

Buddy sat in the back of the auditorium, slumped in his seat. And when it came my turn for first pick, without hesitation I pointed to Buddy. "I want him."

The teacher in charge looked at me and then at Buddy. She smiled at me. "You want Buddy?" she asked. There was no pause in my voice. "I want Buddy."

We didn't win the contest, but we did come in 2nd place. The other members of my team helped convince Buddy that it was "i before e" and charisma started with "ch."

But we lost on the word 'sinecure.' It was an "e" not an "a" in the middle. Oh well, second place wasn't so bad.

The other incident that comes to mind was the day of the final baseball game. Oh how I longed to be chosen and to be on Buddy's team.

Buddy was the pitcher, but Chuckles Flynn was the captain of the team and got to choose the players. Well, neither Little Billy nor I ended up being picked by either team. I laughed and told Little Billy that we had a special position – 'left out,' and he laughed too. Of course, Buddy's team won. He pitched a no-hitter and the final score was 6-0.

And when I walked over to congratulate Buddy amid all his other admirers, Buddy turned to me – to *me*, you hear – and said, "Hey kid, *we* done good."

It would have been wonderful had I been chosen and been part of the winning team. But at least I felt included when Buddy said to me, "we done good." – and I know that Gloria In The Third Row heard *that*!

Many years have since passed and I have learned that life isn't all spelling bees and baseball teams. I often wonder what happened to Buddy, who moved away when he was left back again in the fifth grade.

But I do know what it's like not to be chosen and I'm glad that, in some small way, I beat the system.

Well, just a little.

Assembly Day

"And we recited, 'I pledge allegiance...
and to the country of witches stands...'"

Thursday! Every Thursday was assembly. That meant that all of us third graders would go to the auditorium. There we would sit with the second graders (little guys) and the fourth graders (Wow...WOW...double WOW) and take part in a special hour. Sometimes there would be a guest speaker, sometimes we would listen to records, and sometimes there would be a play or some kind of presentation planned by one of the classes. That was the part I liked the best.

But we're getting ahead of ourselves. First of all, Thursday and Assembly Day had to be planned for. The night before, Mama had to make certain that there was a clean white shirt and a red tie. Of course there were no washing machines and who could afford to send a shirt out? Certainly we couldn't.

So two days in advance, every Tuesday, Mama would wash a shirt. In the warm months it was a short-sleeve and during most of the other school months, a long sleeve. Then the shirt was hung on the clothes line that stretched from the kitchen to the bedroom and we waited for the shirt to dry before taking it off the line. But not too dry – only almost – so that Mama could iron the shirt and hang it on the door knob until Thursday.

Now, I imagine girls had a regimen as well, since they were all required to come to school in skirts and white middy blouses. But my household was all unisex, so girl's attire was not a concern.

Now just in case some of you are wondering what would happen if someone came without the white shirt/red tie, well, don't ask. So you ask anyway, so I'll tell you. No assembly. Instead you sat on a chair outside the office – an outcast, a pariah, a thing of scorn and derision A *nebbish*!

And then in straight lines, the boys on one side and the girls on the other, we entered the auditorium. Of course, each line had a leader and, oh, how we vied for the position and honor. But we marched in, slowly and in absolute silence, and stood in front of the designated chair. Then at a signal from the Principal – an awesome gentleman who stood in front of the auditorium and who controlled our lives (of that, I was certain) – in came the color guard with one of the "big boys" (a sixth grader!) carrying the flag and we all saluted. Those were the days before you placed your hand over your chest. And we recited, "I pledge allegiance...and to the country of witches stands...one nation invisible..."

I didn't know what an "allegiance" was and how then could I pledge it, whatever pledge meant. Witches I knew, but what they had to do with liberty and justice was beyond me. But we never questioned. We recited and then we sang. Oh how we sang, "My country's tears of thee..." until we came to the dreaded line, "Land where my Father died..."

But our fathers were still alive. And somehow I felt it was like reciting the *Kaddish* and to stand and utter those words would bring down the feared Angel of Death, the *Malach Hamaves* to enter our homes.

So to ward off the Evil One, we knocked on wood (the seats in front of us), and whispered or at least silently thought, "God forbid!"

We couldn't take chances, even when the music teacher demanded, "Who's making that noise? What is that tapping? Stop it." But by then the dreaded phrase had passed.

And so we continued. There was the Bible reading (separation of church and state? Ha? Double Ha. Ha-ha!) with all the thee's and thou's and all the words ending in "eth." Somehow the "eth" changed the commonplace every-day word into something sacred and holy, something so very special that we wouldn't dare question.

And then there was the presentation, most of it so inaudible that those of us who sat in the rear missed whatever was said. And we only knew that it was over when we were given the signal to applaud.

Ah, Thursday – Assembly Day. A day set apart from all the rest – the public school "Shabbos." And I look back and smile as I remember the eight year old boy in a white shirt and a red tie and I think – well it was nice being eight and knowing that you could make all the ills of the world vanish by knocking on wood.

If only we could do that today, but...well perhaps...but that's for another story.

A School Wish About "Hitler The Meshugeneh"

"Miss Dugan told the Principal,
"They're all alike."

The year was 1938 and we were all kids growing up in the Bronx. In a few months Europe was going to explode. November of 1938 would signal Kristallnacht, the night of broken glass. Synagogues would be broken into and vandalized. Throughout Germany there would be an explosion of anti-Semitism that would see the smashing of Jewish stores. Swastikas in macabre fashion would appear all over, desecrating Jewish homes, making a mockery of Jewish beliefs and faith. November 1938 would be the prelude to the mass destruction of European Jewry and the beginning of the "Final Solution."

But this was the Bronx and this was the end of summer and school was still out. I heard Mama and Papa talking about the crazy Hitler, the *meshugeneh* of Europe. But their voices were soft, almost whisper-like, and they spoke in Yiddish. They didn't want the *kinder* to understand. But we Jewish kids knew that we had to master the understanding of Yiddish and spelling if we wanted to be privy to all the little secrets of the family. And so we did.

Much of the news was buried in the back pages of the newspapers. The rumors of anti-Semitic purges were less important than the baseball scores and the scandals of the Hollywood personalities. And Papa kept reassuring Mama that this was not a worry. After all, President Roosevelt (this was said as one word, because we never separated the title from the name) would take care of them – of us – of everyone. And so we were satisfied that all was right with the world.

And September followed August. And with September came the beginning of school and first grade (we called it 1-A) and Miss Dugan and more talk of Hitler in whispers that stopped whenever I entered the kitchen, "*Sha, sha –* the child…"

And I worried in between breakfast and lunch and three o'clock milk and cookies (fresh from the oven, still warm) and Mama kept telling me that all was right with the world and I didn't one hundred percent believe her but Papa said that all was right.

But all was not right with the world and somehow, in some peculiar way, my *shtetl* – my turf in the Bronx – was invaded with anxieties and concerns. So I had to consult the authorities. I excluded Mama and Papa because they told me not to be concerned. So that was point…period.

Miss Dugan, my teacher, was next on my list. She knew everything. She knew how to make birthday hats for you to wear on your birthday. She knew how to cut straight lines and to write with a special pen so that the letters would be big and clear.

I asked her about Hitler and she told me that this was not for me to think about. He was an important man in some far off country called Germany (somehow, I thought that it had to do with germs) and that he was helping his people. I was afraid to tell her that my parents called him *meshuga* because I felt she would not welcome this evaluation.

Then she told me to color between the lines and to stop asking questions about things that should not concern me and that I shouldn't make trouble like some people. Who these some people were I didn't know, but I was afraid of them and I didn't want to upset Miss Dugan.

So one *Shabbos* after services, I asked the Rabbi. Now, he should know everything. Who was Hitler and was he helping people? The Rabbi's face turned red and he spit out. "*Pu, pu, pu,*" he said in a hoarse voice and he added some words in Yiddish that with my scanty knowledge I couldn't decipher. But it sounded terrible. I heard the word *meshugeneh* a few times – so he agreed with Mama and Papa – and then he did something that he had never done before. He hugged me and said a blessing. I knew that that was supposed to comfort me, to make all my worries disappear. But they didn't.

And one day in school the Principal came into the room and asked all the children what wish they had for the world. This was the beginning of the school year and we could all make wishes and the children with the best wishes would get rewarded with a commendation card.

And so I thought and thought. Oh, how I should have liked to get a commendation card to bring home and to hang on the wall. Everyone would be so proud of me. Should I wish that Hitler would go away and leave all the germs alone? That would not do. I knew that I better steer clear of world politics.

And so I came up with the perfect wish. When I was called upon, I stood up and said, "I wish that all the boys and girls in the world could have milk and cookies whenever they came home from school at three o'clock and that their mothers would be waiting for them."

Everyone smiled and I saw Miss Dugan reach for the pink commendation card. And then, as if there was some uncontrollable force that took hold of me and forced the words out of my mouth, I added, "and that Hitler would disappear and stop being a *meshugeneh.*"

The smile turned to a scowl. The card was returned

to the desk. I was told to take my seat. Miss Dugan told the Principal, "They're all alike." And he answered, "You're right."

I knew that this was not meant to be a compliment and that somehow I had lost my chance to shine, that Hitler would not go away, and that the vision of the world's children having milk and cookies at three o'clock would fade into the dust.

What happened after that was a jumble. My mother had to go to school, November came, the world turned to shattered glass, and we moved into a new neighborhood where I was enrolled in a different school and placed in a class with a teacher, Miss Jacobson, who had a smiling face that never scowled. And when I told her about the cookies and Hitler, she only held me close to her and said, "I wish for that too. If only…"

She never finished the sentence and it took me many years to know what the "if only" meant.

And by that time… well, you know the rest.

7. Nu? So, What Else Is New?

Mama and the Topic of Condoms

"I could speak easily about the facts of life to my college students...but to my mother?"

It was the moment of truth! I didn't think that this day would come – at least not yet. But I should have guessed. After all, Mama was already ninety-five, so it was time. We had to have a heart-to-heart talk about...you guessed it...(You didn't? So I'll tell you...the facts of life!)

So how did it all begin? Well it started with THE CENTER. You noticed how important those words look? Well to the Ladies (Mama's friends) who sat in front of the building in the warm weather, it was a place to go to ... or not to go to. Fat Rosie From Apartment 3-C spoke up.

"The Center, I don't need. All old people *kvetching* about their aches and pains. Better I could stay *here* and talk about my aches and pains. Why walk three blocks? Just for a free cup of coffee and maybe a prune danish? Not for me."

Her opponent was Lilly With The Hair And The Red Nails. "Rosie, you're an old stick-in-the-mud. You sit in one place like you're glued to the spot. What you need is a change from scenery. And today there's going to be a speaker at three o'clock sharp and afterwards tea with the fancy bakery cookies."

Maybe it was the bakery cookies, but Mama got interested. "So what is he going to speak about? If it's like last month when they had that skinny lady who talked about drugs I'm not interested."

Lilly was quick to respond. "First of all it's not a Lady; it's a man. And in the second place, you loved when the good looking man with the glasses and the sport jacket talked about eating healthy. You remember, you even raised your hand and gave your recipe for blintzes with low-fat cottage cheese. And in the third place what do you have to do today that's so important in the first place?"

Mama was convinced. So she went.

The next day I came to visit. It was raining, so I knew that Mama would be "stuck in the house." First there was the talk about the children, then the weather, then the neighbors and then, "You know yesterday I went with Lilly – well, we went to The Center. In front of the house I can always sit, I figured, and what was to do here? Just gossip about all the people, such nonsense talk. Better I should go where maybe I could learn something. So I went to The Center where they had this nice man who was a speaker and then there was tea and prune danish. They promised bakery cookies, but the woman in charge forgot."

I listened obediently and interrupted almost before Mama could tell me about the prune danish that was too sweet and that one of the women grabbed two and put one in her pocket book wrapped in a napkin. (The danish was wrapped in a napkin, not the pocketbook.)

"Mama," I asked, "what did he speak about? What was his topic?" (Better to talk about that than the danish.)

And then Mama took on a serious expression and she looked me straight in the eye. I tensed. "Yes?" I prodded.

She hesitated for a minute and then asked, "So explain to me, what is a...a...condom?"

I swallowed hard. It was the moment of truth. I could speak easily about the facts of life to my children (well almost easily) and to my college students...but to my mother?…even though – or maybe especially since – she was well past ninety…

This called for some thinking, but I could see that she was waiting for a reply and so I began slowly at first, and looking past that gentle face into the doorway beyond, I explained in simple terms about things like "protection," like "unwanted pregnancies," like "sexually transmitted diseases."

And she listened without interrupting. She didn't seem to be embarrassed when I told her about how important it was for people to "be careful when they…when they…"

I never finished the sentence. After all, there are still some matters that are better off left unsaid. She was past ninety, and as the Bible said about Sara, "well past the way it was with women."

But I thought that I had done a credible job and so I asked, "Any questions?"

Mama smile. "No *Dahling*. That's all very interesting. So smart you are, how you explain things. But still I don't understand one thing."

I closed my eyes and asked, "What is that?"

She didn't lose the smile. "With the condom – how is it different from a co-op? Lilly's daughter wants to move into one of those condoms in Florida and this man never told us the difference."

Condom? Condominium! My eyes were still closed. My lecture on birth control was just another one of those days when I was spinning my wheels until Mama said, "But I liked what you said about being careful. Maybe you could talk at The Center sometime. Only then when you speak, I'll make sure that they have bakery cookies. You can believe me."

And I assured her I did.

The Sweet Smell of Success and Ripe Cantaloupes

"I know you. You're the one who writes.
And the last on was not bad."

Oh the sweet smell of success. The joy of recognition. Enough already. If I keep up like this I'm going to convince myself and then I'll need a new hat size. But yet – a few stories – and all absolutely, positively, one hundred percent true. The *emes*.

I was in the local super market with my wife a few days ago while she was checking out the organic vegetables and the places of origin. She has told me a hundred times, "You can't be too careful. Who knows what they put on these fruits and vegetables to make them grow? Insecticides. Pesticides. All kinds of poisons and then what do we do, we eat them. *Pheh*."

And even though I point out that we always scrub our vegetables and fruits (except maybe bananas), still those insidious poisons manage to invade the peaches and pears and even worse, those beautiful strawberries.

So to continue, while she was lost amidst the broccoli and asparagus, I wandered into the fruit aisle, debating whether I should sample a grape or two or three. I'm not certain whether it was my conscience or my up-bringing. (Tanta Pesha would say, "That's like stealing, unless of course, you're tasting to make sure that the nectarines are sweet, then, of course, it's perfectly all right. Because at such prices to buy the nectarines and then discover once you're home that they have no taste, it's like throwing out money. And that would be a real sin!")

But what decided me was the sign that indicated the grapes had come from some country which did not have strict laws controlling the kinds of sprays that were used – and I couldn't wash the grapes right there in aisle 6-a – that's for sure. That's when I saw this elderly (maybe even a little more than elderly) lady sniffing at the cantaloupes. She looked up and said, "I know you. You're the one who writes. And that last one was not bad. (My article or the cantaloupe? I wasn't certain.) And I recognized that lady you wrote about. She's the one with the husband. I'm right? No? I know her. She keeps herself nice. Always neat and clean. And the husband is always busy with his organizations. I don't know how old she is, but it's hard to tell. She knows how to fix herself good."

I wasn't sure if I should volunteer any information, so I just smiled and basked in her comments.

"I like when you write about the holidays. It makes me think back. But don't talk so much of giving advice to young people. Better they should learn for themselves. And this Fat Rosie From 3-C. She's for real? Or you made her up? I can't remember any yellow building where I lived, but there was a building with a fancy lobby and a canopy. That building you never write about. Maybe you got something against lobbies?"

And here she laughed, so I did too and I assured her that I would write more about buildings with lobbies.

"And my favorite is when you tell about Tanta Pesha. I know she's for real because even my daughter-in-law who spends so much time with her organizations...and better she could dust and clean a little bit…but the children are healthy and after all, what's more important, even my daughter-in-law likes Tanta Pesha, but she says you should tell more about your Bubbie or even your Uncle Max from Memphis."

I was about to promise that I would when she stopped me short.

"So enough already. It was nice talking with you, but if I don't finish my shopping, there will be nothing on the table for dinner and my neighbor who just lost her husband, such a fine lady, I'm going to ask her to come in for a snick-snack."

I asked her her name and apologized that I didn't know her.

"How should you know me? We never met. And for what you need to know my name? We don't know each other. And now let me pick out a good cantaloupe I'll serve for dessert."

And then turning to me she added, "You know something about cantaloupes? How to pick a sweet one, not too ripe, just enough it should have taste."

When I told her that I didn't have any ability with fruits, she gave me a small – very small – smile and turned her back to me, disappearing amidst the cantaloupes while I joined my wife, who had now progressed from the organic veggies to the soy milk.

So, Language Changes

"In those days, all chocolates were Hersheys."

I always liked President Harry Truman. And Mama liked him too. Maybe it was because he was a haberdasher before he entered politics and my father-in-law was also a haberdasher. Or maybe because he was so quick to recognize Israel and welcome her into the family of nations.

But I especially like the story they tell that whenever plain-speaking Harry would be interviewed by the media (I suppose that means the press, since who had TV in those days?), he used the word "manure" quite a bit.

And when one of the Washington Ladies asked his wife Bess if she couldn't try to convince the President to use a more refined term instead of manure, Bess sweetly responded, "It's all I could do to get him to say manure." (We pause for the smile.)

So I remember when Tanta Pesha came over and told us that Lilly With The Hair from upstairs was getting a new refrigerator and Mama said, "So what's so wrong with the old one that I should give the landlord two dollars more a month? It keeps cold and it makes ice. And better the two dollars should be in my pocket than I should give it to that *gonnif* who doesn't even fix the windows that they should close right."

And Mama continued, "But let her enjoy it. I'll even bring up a fresh box of cottage cheese to wish her well with the new ice box."

Ice box? It wasn't an ice box at all. We did our best to try to convince Mama that the days of the ice box were long past and we could hardly remember the time when the ice man came by with those tongs and deposited the block of ice in the...Oh you get the picture. And if you don't, how can I explain?

But as Mama used to say, "You can even teach a cat a new trick." And so finally Mama graduated from saying ice box to saying "frigidaire." It was, "Don't leave the frigidaire open so the cheese will *sperl*." (We couldn't get her to say "spoil" either – it was always *sperl* to rhyme with "earl."

Which she also said like, "Don't use too much *earl* in the *latkes* or they'll be too greasy." And the kitchen floor was covered with – you guessed it, not linoleum – *earl* cloth.

So Mama went up and dutifully admired the new frigidaire and never said a word to Lilly that it was like throwing out money, but rather, "Use it in good health." And then Mama came back to our own apartment and told us that for dessert that night, if we ate our supper good, we would have red Jello.

Now, of course, it wasn't Jello at all because Mama had heard that there was something *trayfe* in Jello, so she used Kojel, which had the seal of approval – and even the nice *rebbitzen* who was such a good cook and who made the most delicious potato *kugel* (you say kigel?) that melted in your mouth – used Kojel and called it Jello. What else?

And in those days a penny was a penny. Today I noticed a penny on the ground and pointed it out to a grandchild, "Look there's money on the ground," and the response was, "It's only a penny." Only a penny! Do you remember when a penny could buy you a Hersheys? All chocolates in those days were Hersheys, even when they were Suchards. (That was the expensive one – two cents at least, but it had an orange flavor and was covered with tin-foil.) But chocolate was chocolate, especially if it was bittersweet and all chocolate was called Hersheys.

And a piece of chocolate was always such a treat! It was given as a reward for a good grade, for doing a *mitzvah*, like bringing the newspaper to the Jewish man on the top floor without even being asked, or when you fell and scraped your knee and Mama washed it with soap and water but didn't have a Bandaid to apply. (Of course it was a Bandaid and not an adhesive strip – we always used the trade name.)

So language changes. But there are still some things. If Mama had lived in the electronic age she would talk about Xeroxing the papers, not duplicating, and she would still say frigidaire. I'm sure of that. You'll excuse me for a minute while I wipe my nose, if you have an extra Kleenex…Ooops.

The Importance Of Asking Questions

*"When I asked her why every conversation
seemed to be concluded with a question,
she said, 'So what's wrong with that?'"*

There's a story I remember. (Yes, my dear reader, I
still remember certain matters; just don't ask me when
I'm supposed to see the dentist or what I ate last night
or even where.) Well, anyway, this story, which may
very well be apocryphal (such a word! So look it
up...just remember it's not Yiddish), concerned Pablo
Picasso (he was the one who drew all the ladies with
three eyes and only one...I better stop) and the writer
Gertrude Stein. (The one who told you that a rose is a
rose is a rose is a...enough already!)

It seems that Stein (no good – the last name doesn't
seem to work here). It seems that Gertrude *(vay iz mir,*
that's even worse, the first name doesn't work at all)
was on her deathbed and Picasso came to her bedside.
She weakly opened her eyes and asked, "Pablo, (for her
it works – first names, that is), Pablo, my friend, what
is the answer?" Then Gertrude Stein (oh well) closed
her eyes and seemed to breathe a last breath. But before
she did, she said, "But better still, more important, what
is the question?"

I like that story, apocryphal (you looked it up?) or
not. There was once an experiment; a group of English
professors (Professors of English? Better?) and a group

of math professors (no problem, here) were asked to grade a set of papers in their respective fields. The result was that there was a greater discrepancy in grades given by the math people than in those arrived at by the – uh – oh – English people (people of English? Naaa.). It seems that the math teachers differed because they were not concerned with the answers, but with the process. This is not be taken as a condemnation of any discipline.

Now Tanta Pesha always knew the importance of questions. In every conversation, she includes such comments as, "You called your mother today?" Or, "Already you're upset?" Or, "A container of milk I should buy?" Or even, "Him you listen to?" And when I asked her why every conversation seemed to be concluded with a question, she said, "So what's wrong with that?"

Nothing at all! In fact, I think that both in the classroom and at home we should encourage the asking of questions – the searching for what is significant – so that our young people continue to ask and not be satisfied with an "easy" response. I think (careful, I'm beginning to sermonize) that students should question not only their professors, but that they should challenge each other, so that, as Hercule Poirot would say, "The little gray cells begin to work."

So I began with a story and so I'll end with one. There were two Yeshiva students who met together. And the first one said, "So go on, ask me a question. I've got such a good answer."

But better he should have said, "Give me an answer. I've got such a good question."

Knowing Good Advice From Bad

"Whenever I'm told something is for my own good, I get nervous..."

A few months ago I was chided by a fellow faculty member. This young woman took me aside after class to offer me a bit of "motherly" advice. To tell the truth, I was (and still am, I suppose) old enough to be her father, but that's beside the point.

"You know," she said with a benign smile. "I hope you won't take what I am about to tell you in the wrong way..." And then she paused. This is always the moment when I begin to worry. Words like "in the wrong way" trouble me.

I prodded her (so to speak), "Yes..."

The smile continued. "I notice that whenever your students leave your room, they seem to be laughing and smiling."

Now normally I should have relaxed and felt good or even perhaps a bit smug. Here I was being complimented. I was being told by a colleague that I had established in my classroom a supportive and pleasant atmosphere, that my students were enjoying the learning experience. Oh sure. Come on now, you heard the "I hope you won't take this the wrong way..." And so I waited for the other shoe to drop.

It did. "This is for your own good," she said. Now that's another phrase that troubles me. Whenever I'm told something is for my own good, I get nervous, and begin to take things the wrong way.

"Learning," she continued is serious. "Our (did she mean mine too?) classroom must be a place where students and professors work together with a serious purpose. There's really no time for laughter and frivolity. No time for bread and circuses."

I almost felt the breath of the lions upon the poor Roman slaves. And I knew that I was one of the poor unfortunate ones and the lion approaching appeared to be in a bad mood, engendered no doubt by having missed a meal.

So what could I do? I thanked her for the advice and asked her not to make mention of this to Stockton College Dean Jan Colijn. I needed the job. I liked to teach. And when you get to be my age, well, it's not easy to find a position. She nodded her head in an understanding way and left.

And I remembered that when I was six years old, I came home and asked my Bubbie for some money. I needed it for the School Fund, I explained. And almost immediately this sweet lady, my Bubbie, dove deep within the pockets of her house dress and took out a handful of coins. "Here take," she said and let me choose whatever coins I needed.

And then she looked at me and without missing a beat added in English that was far from perfect, "Take the money for the school fun. Fun is good in school. Take."

I never explained the difference between fund and fun. There was no need to.

And so when Mama was in her nineties, she was asked if she had any advice for people who wanted to live beyond the "four score and ten." She, too, did not miss a beat. Her answer came quickly. "Every day, have a good laugh – and every day eat a clove of garlic – my advice. Short and sweet."

And so I suppose that the students will continue to laugh. And I hope too they will leave my class with a smile. If not … there's always the garlic.

New Math, New Stockings, and New Batteries

"But if one pair is $3.25, why is three pair $10?"

Suddenly everyone, (So how many is every one? More than five? Don't quibble), everyone (I repeat) is talking about the NEW Math. I'm not at all certain how it differs from the old math, but new must be better – or else why would my wife want to make certain that the soap she purchases is NEW and improved – and my son-in-law tells me that the NEW car has NEW gadgets – and my best friend informs me that I must discard my old ways and develop NEW ideas. So NEW Math must be great. Yes? No! And I am about to prove it to you.

First of all, I must tell you that I was never a mathematics scholar. I majored in English and literature and even a little writing on the side. Of course today, that is really old (aha!) hat; now everyone (more than five) says "language arts" or "humanities."

So I only took the required math courses in college. And my wife, who is a superb Early Childhood teacher, has to take off her shoes when it comes to counting more than ten. (Wait until she reads this; I'll get "what for.") So where in this whole genetic make-up did the two of us together produce a son who majored in mathematics and took courses in Scholastic Processes, Queuing Theory, Quantum Analysis? (I don't even think I'm spelling those words correctly, let alone pronouncing them.) When he did his graduate work, I remember that, one day, when he came home after registration at college, he told me that he had signed up for a course in Elizabethan Literature. And when I told him how thrilled I was that he was finally going to study something that I could relate to, he admitted that it was all a hoax and he was instead going to do work in Pricing Theory and Operations Research.

I threw my hands up in despair. Some more material that I would never be able to relate to — let alone understand.

And so when we went to the Mall last week, all of the above material came together with a vengeance. New Math, Pricing Theory – everything. There at one of the really major department stores (I won't mention names, not even initials… unless you ask.), there was a sign "SPECIAL THIS WEEK."

Immediately our attention was caught. We can never resist a sale or a special. Hosiery was on sale and you can never have enough stockings I am told. (Again I'm not telling you by whom I am told. No names and no initials). And on the very sign it stated, "Three pair for ten dollars."

Knowing very little about hosiery and pricing theory (Ah, so now you see how all this is about to come together) I wondered why on another sign, the message clearly stated, "One pair for $3.25."

Now, I am a product of the OLD math and so I tried to explain to the salesgirl, "Excuse me salesperson, but if one pair was three dollars and twenty-five cents, why should three pair be ten dollars?"

She gave me a haughty look and told me that she didn't set the prices, she only sold the merchandise. And when I persisted in trying to point out that I would save a quarter if I purchased the three pair singly, she, still smilingly, pointed out that she only worked at the counter and she would be glad to show me in black-

and-white how things worked out mathematically, but that her calculator just ran out of batteries.

When I used paper and pencil and multiplied, she maintained that sweet but patronizing smile and said that she never learned long division in high school (Long division? This was multiplication!) and that she always did well with the New Math, but her calculator ran out of batteries and did I want any hosiery? And she gave me a look that seemed to question why did I want to buy ladies' hosiery in the first place? But she was here to wait on customers and not to question their deviant or kinky quirks. I slunk (Hmmnn I never used that word) away and let my wife negotiate the transaction.

The end of the story is that they didn't have the right color in the appropriate size and that was probably why there was such a special sale. When I tried to explain the mathematical fallacy in the pricing, it was too late. We were at the counter where there was a special on lingerie and I decided that sometimes a man has to quit – even when he's not ahead.

And so I leave the lingerie and the New Math to others far wiser and far younger than I. And I fervently pray that their batteries never wear out.

A Moment of Silence...
The Pause That Refreshes

"I expected to get the response that this was the time for creative reflection."

They tell the story that when the Emperor was asked what he thought of the latest symphony composed by Mozart, he replied, "Too many notes." Sometimes that's what we feel when we hear someone rattling on and on without a stop, telling one story after another without even taking a breath. We may feel, "Too many words."

And then there's the case of the husband and wife who had been celebrating their fiftieth wedding anniversary. His guests came by to wish him *mazel tov* and the husband confided, "You know, I haven't spoken to my wife in over ten years." When his guests expressed a mixture of dismay and surprise, the husband continued, "I didn't want to interrupt her."

Which reminds me of a great monologue by Dorothy Parker, "The Waltz." In it she refers to silence as "the sound of angel voices." As a teacher, I think of how often I have ignored that poetic metaphor, choosing instead to opt for nature's abhorrence of a vacuum and rattling on whenever there was that "angelic silence" in my classroom. What happened was, I asked a question and when there was no immediate response, I hastily began to jabber away so that there would be sound in the room.

Perhaps I should have remembered what Mark Twain recalls in his essay, "Memories of a Missouri Farm." He says that whenever a little urchin who was his playmate whistled, it annoyed him, so Twain (who at the time was just a little boy) complained to his mother. She told him that sometimes when children whistle or make sounds it is a distraction for them, and that when there is silence they may possibly be remembering bad or unpleasant experiences. Perhaps she was right; silence may not be dormancy, but an attempt to recall, to organize, to be a kind of pre-oral presentation. And if that is so, then as teachers and parents, we should delight in that silence.

Remember that old Coca-Cola commercial (or was it Pepsi-Cola?) that proclaimed the drink (I know that it was a soft drink advertisement; of that I am certain.) was the "pause that refreshes?" Well, sometimes we need a bit of that refreshment (and now I'm not talking about either cola) in our home and certainly in the classroom.

The poets certainly extol that pause, that moment of quiet reflection. Remember that melody (no, I shall not hum it) of "Love's Old Sweet Song?"

So why shouldn't we? After all aren't we all parental or pedagogic poets? (I didn't even wince while writing that alliterative phrase) I remember that I recently (Is five years recently? I could say four, but...)taught a class in Advanced Methods of Teaching and asked my students, all beginning teachers, what they think of when they hear the phrase "a pregnant pause." I expected to get the response that this was the time for creative reflection. Instead, someone said, "It's that painful silence that follows a question."

My ten year old grandson (He's the attorney; it's his six year old brother who's the brain surgeon. Watch out! Now I'm beginning to tell stories about the grandchildren.) recently asked me if there was anyone in the world who knew more than I. I stopped for a moment, paused and reflected, and then told him that I was certain that there might very well be but that at the moment I couldn't think of anyone.

Then I asked him why he thought I was so gifted. Quickly he responded, "Because you let us think." I didn't continue that conversation. At least, sometimes, I know when to quit when I'm ahead.

And so, dear reader, it is written that Samson slew a thousand people with the jawbone of an ass. If you'll tell me your score, I'll tell you mine...

Yes, Age Is Only a Number

*"There, looking back at me in the mirror
was an elderly – quite elderly – man."*

I'm beginning to worry. Well, maybe "begin" is not the right word, but "worry" hits it right on the head. First of all, I have started to notice that all the policemen are quite young and that when I go to the movies, the very nice cashier doesn't even wait for me to ask for the senior citizen discount. I get it automatically.

I remember how Mama used to feel when once she got on a bus (she was well past eighty at the time) and the bus driver asked her if she was "regular" or "senior." She was so delighted to be asked that she told him she was regular (thank goodness she didn't begin a discussion of the value of a high fiber diet) and she paid full fare – there are times when it's worth losing a few coins.

And then quite recently I went to the Mall because everyone (you know who everyone is) began to "nudge" (not push – nudge) that I needed a new rain coat and there was a big sale (the magic word) on London Fogs.

So I went and tried on a wide variety of coats until everyone (again that word) said the last one was perfect. By this time, I was so tired that I was willing to give the salesman my credit card and take the coat – no matter what – and the sale would have been made.

But, no. The dapper young salesman – salesperson – insisted that I look in the three-way mirror so that I could view my newly about-to-be-acquired elegance. Everyone (aha!) said I should look.

So I looked and ... there looking back at me in a beige London Fog raincoat size forty... there was an elderly – quite elderly – man. I stared at the image. Who? What? I couldn't hear the words of approval. I removed the coat, placed it on the nearest counter and fled. No raincoat. No sale. Everyone (again) looked at me in disbelief. I was behaving like a *meshugeneh* (however you spell that word).

So, where was I? I think I was going to write about the "golden years" and that "age is just a number." But I got side-tracked. I can hear a certain *rebbitzen* (in case you don't know, that's the Rabbi's wife. Of course, you know. Whom am I kidding?) who told me that the time to become concerned is when you get up in the morning and can't remember if today you're going to the doctor or the supermarket.

I like the way I'm invited to join a group of guys at a table in the lunchroom and we have frozen yogurt (I always opt for the no-fat. After all, there are limits). And as we chatter and exchange stories, all those worries that I spoke about in my opening sentence begin to vanish. And then, yes, age is only a number. And all that get-up-and-go that I was so afraid had gotten up and went, suddenly returns.

So maybe I won't meet you on the basketball court for a little one-on-one. But there's still a spring to my walk and I invite you all to join me for a stroll on the Boardwalk.

That is, if you can keep up.

Politics, Religion, and Ruggelach.

"My mouth still waters from the memory."

Fat Rosie From 2-C and Lilly With The Nails were involved in a heated discussion near the stoop when Tanta Pesha joined them.

"So what's all the talk about this time? You're discussing politics or religion maybe?" There was a special little smile curling around Pesha's lips, even as she heard the response. "Politics? Religion? That's none of our business. They're all crooks anyway." (Were they referring to the elected officials or the clergy? You guess.)

And then Lilly piped up, "What should we be talking about? The two most important matters." A pause and then a laugh. "The sales at the market and the doctors."

Fat Rosie took up the slack, "You heard about the Big Market, the one where the girl from the top floor is the check-out? Such a sale! Everything is like half off … even the chickens. Not that I would buy a chicken. But the cream cheese is on special and the jelly without the sugar. Pesha, that's for you when you bake your *ruggelach.*"

Suddenly Rosie's eyes lit up, "*Nu,* and where are the *ruggelach?* My mouth still waters from the memory. It's been a week of Mondays since you invited us in for a *glezzele tay* and some fresh-baked. Maybe you found a gentleman caller who gets the invitation?"

At this there was a giggle. "But not to change the subject, you heard of the new dentist?" Immediately everyone was interested. "Which one? How new?" wondered Rosie.

Lilly explained, "Not new new. Just new. I don't mean the regular dentist – the Lady Dentist – with the smile and the pretty blond girl at the desk, who always makes you feel like you're part of the family – real *mishpacha*. This one is not just a regular – he's a specialist, something with the gums."

All were impressed and urged Lilly on. "So?"

Lilly was quick, "So? So he saved my Shirley's mouth. That's so. And he called her at home to find out how she is and he even stayed late to take care of her. A real *mensch*. And such a sweet face and nice eyes. He looks like a little boy except for the beard."

Pesha became interested, "So, tell me, he's married. No?"

A look of disappointment crossed Lilly's face. "He's married. Yes! And three darling children. So smart, but too skinny."

Rosie looked puzzled. "The children?"

Lilly was fast to explain, "*Oy!* To the wall I'm talking. The dentist."

Rosie gave Tanta Pesha a wink. "Maybe you should go visit him."

Pesha laughed, "So I'll send him my false teeth? Not that it would be such a terrible thing to go see this *metziah* with the golden hands and the eyes. So maybe I'll go when it's time to collect for some disease. Or maybe…"

Then there came a light in her eyes and Tanta Pesha turned to her friends. "So enough already. Tell me, Ladies, there's a sale on the cream cheese and the sugar-free? What better do I have to do tonight. Run for President? So maybe I'll make some of my *ruggelach*, I'll bring over a bunch to your skinny, good looking dentist. And I'll make extra…"

Fat Rosie looked delighted. "You'll make extra for us?"

Pesha began to laugh. I'll make extra for the children." A pause and then, "But what harm if I make extra for us and we can have a couple and talk about politics for a change."

Righteous Gentiles

"This is the way she is paying her back by doing good deeds, real mitzvahs, in her Mama's name."

Tanta Pesha gave me the eye. If you don't quite know what that means, I won't explain.

But the lips curled up and she asked (or should I better say, 'she said'), "So a new jacket you're wearing. Something special, maybe?"

Who could resist answering the good lady? Certainly not I. So I told her, "I've been invited to a party by the President."

Now I have to admit I was hoping that she would fall for this bait and become impressed that I was heading for Washington, D.C. and the Oval Office. But I should have known better. This bait would not even attract a jar of *gefilte fish* and certainly not even a side glance from the Tanta.

But still she appeared to be quite impressed by my good fortune and apparent prestige because she said, "You mean the President from the College (and those words were certainly uttered with capital – not capitol – letters) is making a party and you're going?"

I assured her that this was indeed the situation and inwardly I was pleased that she seemed so pleased, and told her so.

So she told me, "And why shouldn't I be happy? The College President, such a Fine Lady (again all in capital letters), and she invited you (this time a small letter) to come to a party! And this is one Fine Lady (enough with the capitals) let me tell you."

For a minute I was surprised that Tanta Pesha knew the head of our college and I said, "I didn't know that you know..."

I couldn't finish the sentence before I was told, "Know her! *Ayn klaynikite!* I heard her speak more than once even.

"Every year she comes to our *shul* and she tells us of all the wonderful things that the boys and girls are studying. And she's not even Jewish, although she might as well be. And when she comes on the *bimah,* she always says that this is her synagogue. And I know – so you don't have to tell me – how she took care that all the students shouldn't forget about what happened in Europe when that Hitler, a *mamzer ben ha-niddah* – you should pardon the expression – wiped out six million..."

Here Tanta Pesha cleared her throat and for a minute I thought she was finished – but no there was no stopping her. "And you know how she invited people from all over the world, even from Israel, to come and teach. And it's in honor of her Mama – her memory should be for a blessing – that she does this *mitzvah.*"

I was taken aback by all she knew (Tanta Pesha that is, not my President). "Her Mama worked hard all her life," continued Pesha, "doing all sorts of jobs to bring a few extra dollars in the house – no shame in that – and also raising a nice family, and this is the way she is paying her back by doing good deeds, real *mitzvahs* in her Mama's name. And just in case you want my opinion and my two cents, just in case you ask me..."

I knew that there was no need to ask because I would be told, "In case you just happened to ask, her Mama must be looking down and seeing what a good child she raised, and that is a real blessing."

At this point Tanta Pesha reached into the house

dress she was wearing and pulled out a wrinkled Kleenex and started to dab at her eyes which had welled with tears. And if truth be told, I needed a tissue as well and without asking she offered me a spare tissue.

And then Tanta Pesha looked at me, straightened out my tie, patted down my hair, and cautioned me, "So go already. You shouldn't be late. Better you should come early. Maybe you can help out by putting out the silverware or the cups. Make yourself useful."

I thanked her for her good counsel and before I left, kissed her lightly on the cheek. She returned the kiss and gave me an extra hug telling me, "This is for the President, a Fine Lady, make sure you give it to her and tell her it's from Tanta Pesha."

And of course I did.

Even the President Forgets Once in A While.

"My son tells me that if I didn't have my head attached..."

Tanta Pesha was in a dither. So that's a word for the younger generation. For me ... and maybe even for you ... she was *tza-budjet*. (Is that how you spell it? I only say it.) She had been reading the newspaper in the Laundromat, waiting for the wash to dry and bemoaning the fact that in the good old days, you had a clothes line that stretched from the kitchen window to the bedroom window, right over the courtyard. And then you could hang all the clothing and the linens on the line in the fresh air so that when you took everything off the line there was such a smell. A *mechaya*. So good! But what was was and what is is and you have to keep up with the times. So here she was sitting in the Laundromat and waiting.

And so it shouldn't be a total waste, she picked up one of the newspapers and began to read of all the problems that the Poor President was having ... she had just let out a sigh and this nice lady who was sitting next to her asked her what the problem was. Tanta Pesha gave her a weak smile and said, "It's the President."

Her new friend introduced herself. "I'm Jennie from down the block – you know, near the candy store – the building that used to have an awning in front."

A wave of recognition came over Tanta Pesha's face. "The yellow building with the broken sidewalk that they never fix? I know. And I'm Pesha from across the street. I'm just reading here," and she animatedly pointed to the paper, "where the President is having such problems with his memory."

Jennie looked surprised, "You mean the actor President with the wife, who got that disease like Oldhymie's, but he's not the President now."

Tanta Pesha shook her head, "Not that one, this one. What's wrong with you, Jennie? You are maybe a Republican? Anyway I'm not talking politics. Two subjects I don't talk about are politics and religion. How you vote is your affair and how you pray is also your business. I'm talking about how the President forgot where he put all those tapes. So busy he was making coffee for all the foreigners in the White House that he put the tapes somewhere and forgot. Believe me I know the feeling. Not a day goes by when I don't forget where I put something. Yesterday it was the keys and today the pocketbook – the black one with the zipper."

Jennie nodded. She completely agreed. "Me too," she chimed in. "My son says that if I didn't have my head attached ... but who listens to him, the big shot CPA who doesn't have time to call his Mama, even when he knows I have a cold. But I forgot where I put the rent receipt and I thought maybe I threw it out with the garbage. So you're right, Pearlie..."

"Pesha, not Pearlie, and of course I'm right. That's why I know exactly what the President is going through. And everybody is jumping down his throat because he put the tapes down and can't remember where, with all on his mind. I think I'm going to write him a letter and tell him not to worry and to pay no attention to all the people who criticize him because he forgets once in awhile."

Jennie was impressed. "You would write to the President? My goodness, you know his address?"

Pesha began to gather her clothes from the dryer. "Maybe tomorrow. Now I have to put all this together and go home and do some ironing. A maid I don't have and where did I put the pillow cases? You saw a pillow case, Jennie? Did I leave it home or did I come down with it? I'm talking so much I can't keep my mind on one thing. A regular *katz-kopf* I am and I only have the ironing while he has the Arabs and the Cubans and that lady Janet what's-her-name that keeps bothering him all the time."

"Janet?" Jennie asked. "Like Nevada? Isn't she the one who makes the coffees? I get them all mixed up."

"Me too," said Pesha, "but it was nice talking. This is your laundry bag? And look underneath – my pillowcase. See if you look, you find. And that's what I'll tell the President to say."

And off she went to do her ironing.

Those Great Radio Programs We Used To Listen To

"Today we have television and videos and computers...does this stifle imagination?"

On the way to work each day (Again I exaggerate; now that I am in my "silver" years, I work not quite three days a week. But come to think of it, there are meetings and emergencies (like where did I leave my sunglasses, so I can be forgiven). I tune into the radio and try to discover what's going on in the world. Well, of course, the news is enough to depress me, especially when I learn of the latest muggings and carjackings, and now something new on the scene called "road rage."

It seems that there's not enough killings in the world with the crazies who want to use germs and chemicals to blow up their cities, that we have to have some loonies right here trying to act like real *meshugenehs* and kill their parents and then tell the judge that they should be treated with mercy since, after all, they are orphans. Oh where's that book that I'm writing – Six Couches, No Waiting?

So I switch channels and get a Talk Show where the Host (Host? Ha!) is saying that he has an open forum and he should be free to express his opinion, and callers should feel relaxed and express theirs. Then as soon as someone disagrees, you should hear (Scratch that; you shouldn't hear) what the poor caller is called. Since children read this column, I won't write the words, but I can tell you that even in Yiddish I wouldn't say it and if I did Mama would have given me what for and no dessert for a week. And that was letting me off easy. And the music is a cacophony of sounds and then I'm back to the news and the weather and they tell me that it's sunny and clear and I have my windshield wipers going full speed.

So what happened to all those great programs that we used to listen to? Those were the days, believe me, when the children gathered around the radio, not a little three by nothing box, but a big, really big console, that was like a piece of furniture in the living room. And we listened to such good stories. When we were small, there was Let's Pretend, and we heard the dramatization of our favorite fairy tales. That was followed by Grand Central Station, crossroads of a million private lives. And each week we met some new family. So many good stories from Stella Dallas, that poor lady who didn't want her daughter Laurel-baby to learn that she was her real mother. Oy, did she sacrifice for that child. And so did Mary Backstage Noble Wife... or was it Mary Noble, Backstage Wife? Whoever! And Fibber Magee and Molly and The Long (was it Lone?) Ranger and his faithful friend Tonto. (The latter was a Native American, but we called him an Indian since we didn't know better.) And there was even The Shadow. (Who knows what evil lurks in the heart of men. The Shadow knows!) That was my favorite, because no matter how terrible the criminal, how evil and how strong, I always knew that The Shadow would get him and all would work out well. I knew!

And in case you forgot, for Mama and Papa there was WEVD (named after Eugene V. Debbs, but who cares? Not me.) and they had Yiddish programs. Mama's favorite was *"Tzorris bi-Leiten."* I think that you could translate that as Other People's Worries, but it loses a lot in the translation; take my word. The format was always the same. The Old Bubbie who worked all her life for her children and now the Son was married to that awful spendthrift, who didn't care about his family one bit, and told her husband that the Bubbie had to go. She wasn't going to put up with the "Old Biddy" any longer. Such yelling and screaming and weeping. If only I had the Kleenex concession. There was not a dry eye in the room as we listened until we heard "a word from the sponsor." He spoke of an old age home where Bubbie could go and be with people her own age, and eat Kosher meals (You guessed it, the daughter-in-law had no respect for Jewish values or Kosher cuisine.) He made it sound so beautiful. There were even trees outside and benches to sit on with your visitors, if you had any. Believe me, I could bet that the daughter-in-law would never come. And *pu-pu* who needs her anyway!

So today we have television and videos and computers and our children have to see everything. Does this stifle the imagination? Oh well, we've got to be "modren" as Tanta Pesha would say and as Jane Ace from the radio program used to say, "Take the bitter with the better." And as long as they don't take away my memories and leave Tanta Pesha with us, believe me, things could be worse.

My, How Libraries Have Changed!

*"One little seven-year-old smiles at me
and asks if I need help. He'll show me
how to use the computer."*

Each afternoon when school was over and milk and cookie time was completed, there was something special. Today it translates into swimming lessons or karate or soccer practice, but then, it was a bit different.

Of course, Friday meant getting prepared for the Shabbos. Mama had to wash all the floors and then put newspapers on the newly scrubbed linoleum so that the floors would hold on to their shine, at least until the Shabbos had departed. The newspapers were removed just prior to the kindling of the Sabbath candles. But Monday was also special, because every Monday without fail, we went to the "Liberry," that special building that housed a zillion (if not more) books of all types. And all you needed to enter and borrow books was a little card – the library card that helped you to take out books. (No more than two, and only for two weeks at a clip, but you could always renew a book).

To get to the library, you had to walk three blocks and cut across Echo Park – the green spot with loads of rock formations that we used to call "the mountains." (Mountains. Ha! I've seen mountains that would make these look like a valley!) Then came the hard part – we had to cut across two blocks where the "big kids" lived – the kids who went to the "parochial schools" and who didn't wear shirts in the warm weather and who had such menacing looks. And then...and then...came Bathgate Avenue and the "Liberry." What a refuge!

I went straight to the shelves that had the Tom Swift series or to the Jungle Boy books. I had already matured past the fairy tales – the Green Book of Fairy Tales, the Blue Book of Fairy Tales, and the Red Book of Fairy Tales. Tom Swift was great. There was T*om Swift and the Motor Boat* and *Tom Swift and the Secret Message* and *Tom Swift and the*...it goes on and on. Sometimes I even hid one of the books on another shelf if I wanted to save it for another library visit. After all, there were other kids who might be Tom Swift aficionados.

Now I am told that the girls who went to the library made a bee-line for the Nancy Drew or Bobsey Twins books, but that was not my concern. After all, there were limits...

And then came the checkout process. You placed the books on the wooden counter. And the stern-looking librarian – in the brown dress with a collar that came up to her chin, glasses that rested on her nose, and thin lips that never turned up at the corner to evidence a smile – looked first at my card, then at my hands, remarking, "Clean hands before you touch the book."

Then you passed the test. (I always spat on my fingers, wiping them on my pants before entering the library. I knew about the regimen. Word had been passed down from older siblings about the "clean hands" routine). Then, and only then, did you get your books stamped and hear the warning, "Two weeks, not a day late, or else...a FINE."

In spite of all the stern looks and the musty smells, the warnings and the scrutiny, I loved the library then, as I do now. Only now, the library is bright and cheerful, as are the librarians. (Imagine...there are even men who are librarians! And there's a librarian whose name is Miss Joy! And she is just that – with a lovely smile and twinkling eyes…and she plays the guitar for the little children.) And they even have cookies after story hour! (Why, we couldn't even chew gum let alone munch on a wafer in the library!)

And today there are books on tape and videos and newspapers and magazines and comfortable chairs and librarians who say, "Can I help you?" And they mean it! And today they don't tell you "Only two books, no more." (Even though there are still fines for the "overdue" – after all, there are limits to permissiveness. Cookies, yes; tardy….uh-uh.).

But the books are still there and the children come and I join with them and watch as they use the computer. And as I marvel at their expertise, one little seven-year-old smiles at me and asks if I need help. He will show me how to use the computer.

For a minute I hesitate and then say, "Thank you, I'm just looking." But when he offers me a piece of his sugar cookie with chocolate chips, I accept. Not just for me, but for another little boy of years past who worried about his clean fingers and who came to the library on a regular basis and would have loved to munch on a chocolate chip cookie while he was looking for *Tom Swift and the Secret Cave.*

8. Glossary of Conversational Yiddish

(For the "Yiddishly Challenged")

Glossary of Conversational Yiddish
"For the "Yiddishly Challenged"
(With a bissel* Hebrew thrown in.)
*a little bit

A

abee gezunt — as long as you're healthy, as in the expression, "What else matters, *abee gezunt.*" *p. 147*

afikoman — the piece of matzoh that is hidden away to be eaten at the conclusion of the Passover seder. Actually the word is Greek (fooled you, you thought this was all Yiddish!) and means dessert. *p. 164*

a leben af em — long life to him; or more simply "God bless him!" Take your pick. *p. 45, 141*

alta — older or senior. It actually became a name for some people, just as we call someone "Junior." *p. 91* *aroyss vaffen der gelt* — a waste of money (literally, you're throwing out your money on such an enterprise!) *p. 156*

ay-yi-yi — now this expression has several meanings. For example in, "She's not so *ay-yi-yi*, it simply means "so special." But in "*Ay-yi-yi*, do I have a problem!" it means, "Oh my goodness!" *p. 90*

ayn klaynikite — a bit of nothing; or "come on now"; an expression of disbelief or wonder. *p. 210*

ayn und ayntsigeh — "the one and only." Every Jewish child is *ayn und ayntsigeh,* even if he or she has four brothers and six sisters. *p. 76*

a yom tov a freilach — — a joyous holiday, the opening line to a Yiddish song that was sung at Chanukah time. *p. 154*

az mir schmeart fohrt mir — the squeaky wheel gets the grease. (Sometimes it suggests that a little bribe won't hurt!) *p. 71*

a zissin Pesach — a sweet and happy Passover holiday. *p. 164*

B

ballabusta — a woman who is an excellent homemaker. In *Proverbs* we read of the "woman of valor." Now she was a *ballabusta!* *p. 106, 123 bendel* — a little band or a ribbon. A red *bendel* would protect one from the "evil eye." *p. 64*

bimah — the platform or podium in the synagogue. *p. 77, 210*

boichik — simply a "boy," but usually said affectionately, no matter what your age. *p. 83*

boychikel — now this was a "little" boy. The "el" ending is usually the sign of the diminutive. *p. 88*

bris — circumcision. You want to know more, see me after class. According to Jewish law a *bris* takes place eight days after birth and a drop of wine is placed on the baby's tongue. (No wonder Jewish men don't become alcoholics! Think of the association!) *p. 87, 90*

bubbie — grandma. Such a lovely word! *p. 32, 75, 76, 146*

C

chaleryas — pestilence or cholera. But when a woman is called a *chalerya* she is a vixen, a termagant, a shrew, a "chalerya!" *p. 69, 109*

chanukiah — the eight branched candlestick used during the festival of Chanukah. *p. 153*

chatschka — a bauble; a trinket; a nik-nak. (Mama called them nok-niks.) *p. 39, 119, 121*

chometz — bread; and by extension, all foods prohibited during Passover. *p. 163*

D

dayenu — enough! The popular refrain of a song that is sung during the Passover celebration. *p. 164*

der tochter fun shylock — Shylock's daughter; the Yiddish rendition of Shakespeare's *Merchant of Venice*. *p. 109*

der emes — the truth; or the equivalent of "I swear to God!" *p. 110*

der gantze velt iz a tay-ater — the whole world is a theater! Or as the bard said, "All the world's a stage!" And he wasn't even Jewish! *p. 109*

der koenig lear — King Lear, as in the Shakespearean tragedy by the same name. *p. 69*

dos iz der emes — it's the truth! *p. 109*

dreidel — the little spinning top played with on Chanukah, with four letters informing us that "A great miracle happened there!" *p. 109*

E

emes — you already learned this. See *der emes. p. 64*

F

far vuss nit — so why not? *p. 98*

finster vee drerd — as dark as H--l! (This may be a family book, so I am being careful.) *p. 138*

freilach — happy; joyous; Another nice word. *p. 154*

funferrer — actually, this originally had the connotation of someone who nasalized his speech and talked through his nose. Then it took on the meaning of a "deceiver" or a "goof-off" or even a "double-talker." *p. 91*

fun gornisht kumt gornisht — a line from *King Lear*, only in Yiddish. "Nothing comes from nothing!" *p. 69*

G

gefilte fish — Jewish "soul food." Oh come on now, surely you must have eaten this "delicacy." Now-a-days you can buy it in any supermarket, but when I was a boy… *p. 163, 209*

gelt — money. *p. 154*

genuge shoyn — enough already. *p. 12*

geshtorben — Dead, as in "dead." *p. 61*

geshrai — a loud outcry; a scream; a yell. *p. 24, 161, 166*

gevalt — now this was a *geshrai* and means something more than "goodness gracious." *p. 161*

glezzele — a little glass. Did you spot the diminutive ending here? Good for you! *p. 85*

glitzeeyanas — Jews from Galicia, a province of Poland or Austria. They were often at odds with the *Litvaks*, Jews from Lithuania. *p. 148, 154*

gonnif — a thief! Sometimes it is used affectionately when a child is called a *gonnif,* but don't bet on it. *p. 191*

gornisht — nothing. *p. 69*

greener couziner — the green horn, someone newly arrived in America and not yet a "Yankee." *p. 165*

grivenes — when chicken fat was rendered with some onions and a dash of garlic (What else?) this was produced, a high cholesterol, multi-caloric spread. Try it on rye bread, if you dare. *p. 73*

groggers — noisemakers, not the people kind but the little toys that kids use to make sounds. On Purim time you used your grogger every time that the villian Haman's name was mentioned. Booooooo! *p. 162*

grub yung — a boorish individual; a coarse or uncouth fellow. *Pheh! p. 138*

gutteh neshomeh — a good soul. This is a high compliment. *p. 142*

H

haimish — a down-to-earth person, one who doesn't put on airs; literally a "homebody." *p. 150* *hamantaschen* — a delicacy! A three cornered cookie filled with prune butter (lekvah) or jam or raisins and .... enough already. It was thought to resemble the hat that the no-goodnik Haman wore. In Israel it's called oznai haman, or Haman's ears. Take your pick. But both are yummy. *p. 162*

ha-tikvah — literally "the hope." This is the title of the Israeli National Anthem. *p. 153*

havdallah — the ceremony that takes place on Saturday evening at sunset to signal the departure of the Sabbath and the beginning of the regular work-week. *p. 48*

K

kaddish — literally "sanctification," but usually thought of as the prayer recited by those in mourning. *p. 182*

katz-kopf — literally a "cat in one's head," but it usually means a forgetful person. *p. 214*

keppie — a diminutive for "head" so we might say "a blessing on your keppie (head)." *p. 48*

kiddush — the blessing over the wine. *p 106, 107, 148*

kinder — children; the plural of *kind*. *p. 111*

k'nine a hara — An imprecation to keep away the evil eye. Nobody, and I mean *nobody,* wants to get a *k'nine a hara! p. 63, 64*

knish — now this is a delicacy that you should try. It's a pastry dough filled with potato, or meat, or kasha, or whatever. *p. 167*

kristallnacht — the "Night of the Broken Glass," that infamous day in Nazi Germany in November 1938 when synagogues were broken into and Jewish store fronts were shattered and vandalized. *p. 111*

krychick — the end of a loaf of bread; that crusty corner. Mmmmnnnnn. *p. 89*

kugel — a pudding. Sometimes there's a potato kugel and sometimes a noodle (or *lokshen*) kugel, but who cares? They're both delicious. *p. 33, 166, 192*

kvetching — complaining or whining. Many a husband has told his wife (and vice-versa), "Stop your kvetching!" *p. 140, 185*

L

lamed vovnik — tradition has it that the world exists because of 36 righteous individuals and each is called a "lamed vovnik." Lamed-vov are the two Hebrew letters that add up to thirty-six. *p. 43*

langer — tall or long. *p. 91*

lashon rah — or better yet, *loshon hara*. Literally a "bad tongue"; slander or gossip. To be avoided like the plague. So take care. *p. 149*

latkes — pancakes made with oil and grated potatoes. Ask and I'll send you a recipe. Usually eaten at Chanukah time, but who cares when? *p. 192*

litvak — a Jew from Lithuania. See the word *glitzeeana. p. 148, 154*

loksh — a noodle; a tall skinny guy! *p. 91*

l'shana tova tikatayvu — may you be inscribed in the Book of Life for a good year; the traditional greeting on Rosh Hashana, the Jewish New Year. *p. 146*

M

macher — a person of influence; or at least someone who thinks he or she is such a person; a big shot. And if you want to make this the superlative say, *a gantzeh macher. p. 12*

ma-oz tzur — *Rock of Ages.* A traditional song sung on Chanukah. *p. 154*

malach hamaves — the angel of death. So beware! *p. 182*

mamzer ben ha-niddah — *Oy,* is this an expression! Don't use it lightly. It means a "bastard that was conceived during the time the mother had her period." I warned you in advance to be careful! *p. 210*

mann tracht und gott lacht — "man plans and God laughs" or "man proposes and God disposes." *p. 35*

matanah — a gift. *p. 150*

maxele — diminutive for Max as in Maxie. *p. 81*

mazel tov — surely you know this. "good luck!" or "congratulations!" *p. 169, 201*

mazel — luck. *p. 147*

me y'malel — a popular Chanukah song; "Who can retell" *p. 154*

mechaya — a pleasure; a delight! *p. 212*

meese — ugly, plain in appearance. *p. 91*

meese n'shumeh — an ill-favored person; not a nice person. The opposite is a *gutteh neshomeh. p. 137*

mensch — a real good person; a fine human being. In short, a *mensch. p. 207*

menshlichhkeit — the practice of all the virtues befitting a person. *p. 99*

meshuga — crazy; stupid! *p. 112*

meshugenas — zanies; silly or crazy people. *p. 63*

meshugeneh — This is the singular. One is enough! *p. 111, 113, 205*

metziah — a find! a treasure! *p. 207*

minyan — a religious quorum. It takes ten men to make a *minyan* in traditional Judaism. *p. 103* *mishpacha* — family. But when you say "the whole mishpacha," you mean EVERYONE, related or not! *p. 163, 207*

mit schlag — with cream, usually whipped cream or as Mama called it "whip-cream." Not for the calorie-conscious...even in Yiddish or Viennese.. *p. 20*

mit-vokch — the middle of the week. I suppose that that's Wednesday. *p. 76*

mitzvah — a good deed; literally a "commandment" since God commands us to perform good deeds. *p. 68, 95, 120, 142, 193, 210*

mogen david — the six pointed Star of David. *p. 151*

mohel — a person who performs circumcisions. How's that for a profession?! *p. 88*

N

narashkeit — nonsense. *p. 161*

nebbish — a wimp; a bit lower than a *schlemiel*; could also be used as an interjection conveying the idea of "alas!" *p. 182*

nisht by unz gedacht — God forbid! *p. 106*

noch — yet; even; (surprisingly). *p. 11*

nosh — a snack, a bit of food taken between meals. "Have a *nosh* before dinner!" *p. 58 nu?* — Next to *oy*, the most frequently used expression. It means, *So...? p. 93, 206*

O

ois-ge-pitzt — all dressed up, probably in a fancy over-dressed outfit. *p. 87*

oneg — Actually it means "joy" but has come to be associated with the refreshment taken after a religious service. *p. 61, 82*

or-mayn — the Yiddish equivalent of *Amen*. *p. 147*

oy — now here is the most frequently used expression. Just heave a sigh and say, "*Oy!*" Much better than the pallid "Oh!" Just ask any Jewish mother. *p. 23, 25, 67, 84, 117, 122, 124, 144, 166, 207*

oy vay — double *OY! p. 88, 163, 193*

oy chanukah, oy chanukah, a yom tov a freilach — a yiddish song. The translation is "Oh Chanukah, Oh Chanukah, a happy holiday!" But in Yiddish it's so much better! *p. 154*

oyz — plural of *oy*. If one *oy* is good then two is... *p. 163*

P

pekel — a little package (There's that diminutive again!); a little bit of something. *p. 71*

pheh — *Pheh* is pheh! Like *pu-pu-pu*, only *pheh*; a sound of disgust. *p. 67, 74, 84, 94, 103, 148, 188*

pisk — a not so nice expression for the "mouth" (cf. French "guele") *p. 165*

ponim — face. *p. 48*

pu, pu, pu — the sound of spitting out. See the notation under *pheh*. *p. 64, 113*

pupik — The belly-button or navel (are you an in-zy or an out-zy?) *p. 88*

Q

quvell — to experience a sense of inner (and even outer) pride, usually in one's children. What else? A synonymn, sort of, for to *tschepp nachos p. 12*

R

rebbitzen — the Rabbi's wife. *p. 98, 159, 192, 205*

ruggelach — a delicious cookie rolled up and stuffed with raisins and nuts. You must taste one to appreciate it. So have a *nosh. p. 118, 206*

S

schlumpy — ill kempt; sloppy, slovenly. *p. 107*

shandeh — a shame! *p. 26, 109*

shayne — pretty *p. 56*

shikkur — a drunk; intoxicated. *p. 88, 151*

shivah — literally, Hebrew for "seven." This usually conveys the idea of the seven days of mourning following the death of an immediate member of the family. *p. 65, 152*

shlep — to drag along, to pull. A person who is a *shlep* is a jerk, a wimp, an unkempt drip. *p. 109*

shlepping — see *shlep* and you have the idea. *p. 40, 68, 141*

shlumpy/shlumper — slovenly; ill-kempt. *p.43, 107*

shmateh — a rag; something your ex-husband's new girlfriend wears. *p. 67*

shmeared — spread; Also used to indicate a bribe. *p. 66*

shmearar — one who paints, but not too carefully. *p. 84, 85, 86*

shmooze — idle talk; chit-chat *p. 141*

shmutz — dirt. *p. 148*

sholem — a favorite word, from the Hebrew meaning "peace." What could be better? *p. 160 shtetl* — a small community of Jews, usually reminiscent of the small towns in Poland before the Holocaust. *p. 110, 112*

shtick nachas — a special bit of joy. Every child is a *shtick nachas* to his grandparents. You don't believe this? Ask my wife! *p. 48*

shul — a synagogue. *p. 48, 82, 94, 103, 144, 151*

simcha — a joyous or happy occasion, a celebration. *p. 151*

sufganiot — jelly donuts. Just go to Israel at Chanukah time and you will eat plenty! *p. 152, 153*

T

taiglach — a confection made with honey and raisins and nuts and then more honey. Usually eaten on the Jewish New Year. *p. 150*

takkeh — really; "you're not kidding me." *p. 160*

tallis — a prayer shawl. *p. 88*

tallisim — plural of *tallis*. *p.146*

tanta — aunt. *p. 80, 89*

tattele — a boy-child is a tattele, a little daddy and a girl is a mammele. But both are chips off the old block, but Jewish ones! *p. 56*

trayfe — not kosher; forbidden. *p. 57, 91, 138, 192*

tsorris — troubles, worries; concerns. We all have them, so learn the word! *p. 110*

tsorris bi-leiten — other people's problems. This was the theme of a popular radio (you remember radio?) program. *p. 216*

tushie — a rather endearing term for that part of the anatomy on which we sit, probably a corruption of *tuchis*, which was a bit off-color. You could pinch (or even kiss) a child's tushie, but you gave him or her a *potch* (slap) *in tuchis!* *p. 21, 25, 26*

tza-budjet — discombobulated; mixed up; confused, but with a "capital C." *p. 212*

tzedaka — charity *p. 20*

V

vay iz mir — "woe is me." But in Yiddish, of course it's so much better! *p. 64, 87, 108*

Y

yarhtzeit — the date marking the yearly anniversary of someone's passing. There are candles in glasses that are usually used as a memorial. *p. 82*

yarmulkes — the skull caps worn by men in a synagogue *p. 48, 100*

yenta tallabenta — a gossip; a chatter-box (I know this is sexist, but it refers only to women). *p. 148*

yeshiva — a Jewish day school for Orthodox boys. *p. 100*

Yiddishkeit - a sense of things Jewish. After yiou read this book you will have a real sense of *Yiddishkeit. p. 11*

yom tov — a holiday. *p. 87, 150, 151*

Z

zaydies — plural of *zaydie*, a Grandpa! *p. 63, 75, 76, 146*

zoll gornisht helfen — nothing can help. It's a *fait accompli!* How's that for mixing languages? *p. 72*

zibitel — from the word meaning "seven" Usually, when there is a premature birth or one that comes "too soon" after the official marriage, the baby is called a *zibitel*. Aha! *p. 90, 92*

zissen — sweet. *p. 164*

Looking for a great gift?

Send *everyone* *you* *love* a copy of

Memories of
Laughter & Garlic

Qty	Title	Price	Total
	Laughter & Garlic	**12.95**	
	Shipping & handling Add 3.00 for first book & $2.00 for each additional book		
	Sales tax (NJ residents only add 6%)		
	Total enclosed		

Name _____

Address _____

City _____ ST_____ Zip_____

Daytime Phone ____(_____)_____

E-mail _____

(Please enclose any additional mailing addresses on a seperate sheet)

Make check payable to:
ComteQ Publishing
P.O. Box 3046
Margate, NJ 08402

Thank you for your order!